TRUMP
America First

TRUMP
America First

COREY R. LEWANDOWSKI
and DAVID N. BOSSIE

CENTER
STREET®

NEW YORK   NASHVILLE

Center Street
Hachette Book Group
1290 Avenue of the Americas, New York, NY 10104
centerstreet.com
twitter.com/centerstreet

First Edition: September 2020

Center Street is a division of Hachette Book Group, Inc. The Center Street name
and logo are trademarks of Hachette Book Group, Inc.

The publisher is not responsible for websites (or their content)
that are not owned by the publisher.

The Hachette Speakers Bureau provides a wide range of authors for speaking
events. To find out more, go to www.HachetteSpeakersBureau.com
or call (866) 376-6591.

Print book interior design by Timothy Shaner, NightandDayDesign.biz

Library of Congress Cataloging-in-Publication Data has been applied for.

ISBNs: 978-1-5460-8492-1 (hardcover), 978-1-5460-8529-4 (large type),
978-1-5460-8606-2 (signed edition), 978-1-5460-8605-5 (BN.com signed edition),
978-1-5460-8493-8 (ebook)

Printed in the United States of America

LSC-C

10 9 8 7 6 5 4 3 2 1

To Our Families and

The Silent Majority—MAGA

CONTENTS

★

TRUMP
America First

★

I want all Americans to understand: we are at war with an invisible enemy, but that enemy is no match for the spirit and resolve of the American people...

...It cannot overcome the dedication of our doctors, nurses, and scientists — and it cannot beat the LOVE, PATRIOTISM, and DETERMINATION of our citizens. Strong and United, WE WILL PREVAIL!
                        —@realDonaldTrump, March 18, 2020

Let's face it. Donald Trump is a rough individual. He is vain, insensitive and raw. But he loves America more than any President in my lifetime. He is the last firewall between us and this cesspool called Washington. I'll take him any day over any of these bums. #Trump2020
                        —@realJamesWoods, May 17, 2020

★

CHAPTER ONE

JUST WHEN YOU THINK YOU'VE SEEN EVERYTHING

The world of politics, it turns out, isn't immune to a global pandemic. If you told us that a Chinese virus would circle the globe, crash the stock market, kill over one hundred and forty thousand Americans, and bring both President Donald J. Trump's and former vice president Joe Biden's presidential campaigns to a screeching halt, we would have told you you've read one too many Stephen King books, which you shouldn't be doing, by the way, seeing he's a Trump hater.

And yet, here we are.

We have been lucky enough to visit the president in the White House often but never quite like the experience we had on May 18, 2020. We were both still home with our families waiting for the Covid-19 crisis to end when the president called Corey and asked him and Dave to come see him at the White House. Molly Michael, the president's Oval Office operations coordinator, followed up to book our appointment for 11:30 a.m. but added a small detail at the end of the call. She told us we would need to be at the Secret Service checkpoint outside the West Wing at 10:30.

Corey flew down from New Hampshire; Dave drove in from his home in Maryland. Neither of us knew exactly why we had to be at the checkpoint so early. As we pulled up to West Executive Drive just outside the White House we had our answer—you couldn't miss it. There, in front of the checkpoint, were two newly erected clear medical tents.

Welcome to the White House in the age of coronavirus.

———————

As of this writing, the coronavirus has caused a countrywide lockdown, and millions of hardworking Americans to become unemployed. The world's greatest political apparatus, the 2020 Trump-Pence reelection campaign, has almost entirely transitioned to a virtual operation. The campaign headquarters in Virginia has been closed. Rallies, the lifeblood of the campaign, have been put on an indefinite hold. Wall-to-wall news coverage of Covid-19 has drowned out campaign advertising across all platforms. It was like nothing we had seen before, and in politics, at least, we've seen a lot.

So now, in the middle of campaign season and after almost five non-stop years of being on the road fighting for the president of the United States, doing everything in our power to first get him elected and now reelected, we've found ourselves in the one place neither of us ever expected: Home.

Historians will look back on the Trump 2016 presidential campaign as the most incredible political comeback ever. Corey was the president's first and longest-serving campaign manager. With Corey guiding the 2016 operation, candidate Trump won thirty-eight primaries and caucuses and received more votes than any candidate in the history of the Republican primary process. Dave has been one of the president's most trusted outside political advisors longer than just about anyone else. He joined the 2016 effort as deputy campaign manager in August and steered the campaign down the furious stretch to victory.

We're also the authors of *Let Trump Be Trump: The Inside Story of His Rise to the Presidency,* the number one bestselling account of the 2016 presidential race that even the most liberal news outlets call the seminal work of that historic ride. With a tsunami of outside factors threatening to blow this presidential election cycle sky high, the 2020 campaign has become the most important race in American history.

Still, as much as we love our wives and children, sheltering in place got old. For guys like us, for whom politics is the very air we breathe, you might as well have told us the country has turned socialist and all elections have been called off (take it easy, AOC, it's only an analogy).

Don't get the wrong idea. It's not as though we were just sitting home feeling sorry for ourselves; we worked the phones as hard as ever. In January 2020, Dave was named Maryland State cochairman of the Trump-Pence reelection campaign, and he served as the vice chairman of the Republican National Convention. At the end of March, along with his cochair in Maryland, Congressman Andy Harris, he conducted a conference call with hundreds of Trump volunteers from across the state. Dave asked then Trump campaign manager Brad Parscale and Chris Carr, the political director, to say a few words on the call. Brad told the volunteers about the challenges of running a campaign in the days of Covid-19. He explained how the leadership team was transitioning much of the reelection effort to the virtual realm. Chris Carr then emphasized the need for the volunteers to join the virtual effort and to work the phones as though the reelection depended on it.

Corey, a senior campaign advisor for the president's 2020 reelection effort, is making his cell phone carrier sorry it gave him an unlimited data plan. Corey is serving as the chairman of the Trump Victory Team for New Hampshire and served as the chairman of the New Hampshire delegation to the Republican National Convention. Corey organized a similar call for the Trump team in New England with campaign volunteers.

We'd also been in constant contact with the president, including meetings in the Oval Office, where we gave him our frank assessments of the state of his reelection effort, specifically regarding the data from important swing states. Still, not being out on the campaign trail, a tradition of American politics since before Abraham Lincoln made all the whistle-stops from Springfield to DC, has been frustrating, to say the least. And it's frustrating on a couple of levels.

For one, as confident as we were in the team's ability to take the overwhelming percentage of the campaign online, the Trump rally is something that can never be virtually duplicated. Later in this book, we'll take you inside and backstage at rallies so you can see for yourself the energy and importance they hold. As with Twitter, the rallies give the president the opportunity to take his message directly to the American people. But unlike Twitter, rallies give the American public the chance to see the energy and love this president has for the country firsthand. That's something you can't replace.

The other reason we're frustrated is because the virus lockdown is keeping Joe Biden in his basement and out of the public eye. As nonexistence is where he's at his best, the former VP can continue to hide the fact that he's not fit for office and keep his poll numbers artificially high, all while being cheered on by his allies in the mainstream media. President Trump, on the other hand, is confronting a once-in-a-century pandemic, has begun to navigate the economy out of the unprecedented fallout from the virus, and faced perhaps one of the hardest decisions an American president has ever had to make: to close down the greatest economy the world has ever seen, which he built in three short years, in order to slow the spread of the virus.

———————

From the beginning of the Covid-19 pandemic, President Trump has made the right choices. While House speaker Nancy Pelosi and Democrats in the House were debating whether to allow the sale of flavored tobacco—which was the only piece of legislation allowed onto the floor during the month of February—President Trump was working with the Coronavirus Task Force, led by Vice President Mike Pence, to stop the "invisible enemy" from spreading. They recruited the best private companies in the world to develop and produce tests, provide crucial ventilators and masks, and to send the message that the United States of America would reopen for business as soon as possible.

During White House daily briefings, President Trump invited experts such as Dr. Anthony Fauci, the director of the National Institute of Allergy and Infectious Diseases, and Dr. Deborah Birx, US global AIDS coordinator and US special representative for global health diplomacy, to speak directly to the American people and share important information that every American needed to know. These experts reassured the public that the government was executing a plan to keep them safe.

Whenever governors asked for assistance, regardless of party affiliation, President Trump delivered. When Democrat governor Andrew Cuomo of New York went on television requesting the president provide New York with hospital beds, President Trump dispatched the Army Corps of Engineers to turn the Jacob K. Javits Convention Center on Manhattan's West Side into an army field hospital. While Governor Cuomo was on television yet again, claiming the victory as his own, President Trump arranged for the USS *Comfort*, a naval hospital ship, to dock in Manhattan to alleviate any potential overcrowding issues. When California's Democrat governor, Gavin Newsom, made similar requests, the president was there. Not only did he help deliver hospital beds, but he also ordered the USS *Mercy* to San Francisco to provide medical assistance.

Thankfully, because of the swift actions of the president and his team, many of those facilities were underutilized.

In fact, many of the states that predicted doom and gloom, forcing people inside and shutting down their economies, were some of the hardest hit during the pandemic. It's no accident that cities with Democrat leaders such as New York City, Detroit, and Chicago are going to be crawling back from the economic disaster they've wrought for decades. The leaders of those cities opted for hysteria instead of good science. When they had the chance to take a good, honest look at the risk and react accordingly, they failed.

In New York, Governor Andrew Cuomo shut down the state and put hundreds of thousands of people out of work. A few days later, he signed an executive order that required nursing homes in New York to admit patients who'd been infected with Covid-19. As a result, thousands of people died unnecessarily in nursing homes in the state.

In New Jersey, Democrat governor Phil Murphy also forced businesses to close. But he went notably further, dictating how people could live their lives: he told them when they were allowed to go out, when they could go shopping, and when they were allowed to go for a walk in the park. When Fox News host Tucker Carlson asked him whether his actions were constitutional, Governor Murphy said that he "hadn't been thinking about the Constitution" when he'd put his orders into place. At least he was honest.

Florida, by contrast, handled the pandemic differently. At the very beginning of the pandemic, the internet was flooded with pictures of students on spring break declaring that they didn't care whether they got the virus or not. For a few days, the media inundated us with those images, warning that Florida was going to be the next Italy or New York. Republican governor Ron DeSantis, an independent-minded conservative, decided not to listen to the Fake News. He did not close down the state the way Governor Cuomo did in New York, and he made sure that vulnerable populations such as people in nursing homes—of which there are many in Florida—were protected.

In Georgia, Republican governor Brian Kemp also kept his state mostly open during the pandemic. He put measures into place only until the people in his state "flattened the curve" and then quickly reopened once the risk of infection went down again. He knew that as bad as Covid-19 was, the economic damage that would be done by forcing businesses to stay closed would be much, much worse.

"Our analysis shows quite clearly," he said as the state was about to reopen, "that states that open up the soonest and the safest—and Iowa and Oklahoma and Georgia are three examples of states that are doing that—will have much swifter and stronger recovery than states that stay closed."

Republican governor Kristi Noem of South Dakota never closed any businesses or issued a shelter-in-place policy for her state. Instead, she went on the offense. By focusing on personal responsibility, the people of South Dakota were able to continue to earn a living without government picking winners and losers as it did in so many other places. Further, in partnership with the three major health care systems in the state, she initiated the first state-backed statewide clinical trial on the use of the malaria drug hydroxychloroquine as a therapeutic.

Of course, the press will never give governors such as Noem, Kemp, or DeSantis credit for their leadership. As with anything else, whatever President Trump and Republicans did during the crisis was the wrong thing—even when they were absolutely correct—and whatever Democrats did was right. When President Trump announced, just hours after we had left a meeting with him in the Oval Office, that he'd been taking hydroxychloroquine as a prophylactic measure against the virus, the media went insane. They cited studies that said the drug could kill people. The Fake News warned that anyone else who died as a result of taking hydroxychloroquine would be dead because of President Trump's dangerous rhetoric.

But as usual, President Trump had been right all along. According to the *New York Times*, the authors of two studies that said drugs such as hydroxychloroquine were dangerous were forced to retract their research because "the authors could not verify the data on which the results depended." Those were the people you were supposed to trust, the so-called experts you had to listen to or else you'd be called "antiscience." Boy, how things change.

President Trump was correct about the virus, hospital beds, ventilators, hydroxychloroquine, and reopening our economy. He was also correct about the fact that the stock market was going to roar back in no time. Well, it's already back.

From the onset of the pandemic, President Trump demonstrated strong and unwavering leadership skills. Revisionist historians in the leftist media would have you believe that everyone outside the administration knew what the coronavirus held in store for the United States. By the end of February 2020, the Chinese Wuhan virus had had a limited impact on the United States and there was little to worry about, according to the so-called experts. However, looking to prevent any potential problems, President Trump showed leadership on the issue in late January. He banned travel from China, a move that potentially saved hundreds of thousands of American lives and that Joe Biden thought of as "xenophobia." He assembled the Coronavirus Task Force, which provided national leadership on the issue for months to come, and declared the virus a public health emergency. Don't believe the Fake News. The president and his administration took swift and decisive action as soon as coronavirus appeared well ahead of any warnings from the "experts."

A virus like this had not hit our shores in more than one

hundred years. Yet while the president continued to do everything in his power to bring down the "invisible enemy," the mainstream media were busy rewriting their own history with the coronavirus. While they falsely accused the administration of not taking the threat of the virus seriously enough in the beginning, they said that they, the great bastions of journalism, had been warning Americans all along. They did warn us, but not in the way you might think. Telling us not to worry or make too big of a deal over coronavirus was their only message—no nuance, no debate. The president's press secretary, Kayleigh McEnany, exposed the media's hypocrisy at a May 2020 press conference. She asked such Goliath-biased news organizations as the *Washington Post*, the *New York Times*, National Public Radio, and others if they wanted to take back the headlines they published downplaying the threat of the virus. Here are just a few:

"WORRIED ABOUT CATCHING THE NEW
CORONAVIRUS? IN THE U.S., FLU IS A BIGGER THREAT"
—NPR, January 29

"WHY WE SHOULD BE WARY OF AN AGGRESSIVE
GOVERNMENT RESPONSE TO CORONAVIRUS"
—The *Washington Post*, February 3

"IN EUROPE, FEAR SPREADS FASTER THAN THE
CORONAVIRUS ITSELF"
—The *New York Times*, February 18

Not exactly Paul Revere, were they?

It would be laughable if those stories from January and February 2020 hadn't downplayed the very real threat to the American people the virus posed. It was journalistic malpractice at its worst. There was no accountability among the press—only more false accusations and shifting of blame.

Once it became evident that Covid-19 could not be contained, the president rapidly expanded coronavirus testing. He made sure hospitals across the country had the resources and protective equipment they needed, including many more ventilators than were ever used. In addition to the Javits Center in New York, he ordered the Army Corps of Engineers to build emergency field hospitals in Detroit, Miami, Denver, and other cities at the cost of $660 million, with most ending up not treating a single patient. He pushed Congress to pass economic relief legislation to save small businesses and put much-needed cash into the pockets of the American people. He directed billions of dollars to private medical research and development to fast-track therapeutics and a possible vaccine. And he did all that while the entire Democrat Party and its allies in the media were unleashing an unending torrent of misinformation and outright lies about him.

Meanwhile, as the Covid-19 crisis wore on, the greatest economy the world has ever seen, one that President Trump had built out of the ruins of the Obama administration, was stretched to its limit. In one ear, he had a chorus of medical experts recommending closing the country, liberal Fake News blowing everything out of proportion, and the Democrat Party doing its best to take down Donald Trump and ruin as many American lives as it could in the process. Hollywood elitist and talk show host Bill Maher even said, "I think one way you get rid of Trump is a crashing economy. So, please, bring on a recession. Sorry if that hurts people."

In the other ear, he had the voices of millions and millions of Americans who were out of work and losing hope, businesses large and small pleading for him to open up the economy, and a volatile stock market that was putting everyone's retirement savings at risk.

For the Democrats, the president's quandary was a dream come true. After so many failed attempts—the phony Russian investigation by Special Counsel Robert Mueller, the outrageous abuse of congressional power with the impeachment hearings, and millions of untruths told and written by the coastal elites—they thought they finally had him where they wanted him. If he held back the economy, he didn't care about American livelihoods. If he opened the economy, he didn't care about Americans' lives. No matter what he did, they would blame him.

In the face of it all, day after day, President Trump stood in front of the hostile press and reassured the public of the strength of America's character. At each press conference, he promised the American people that we would get through the crisis together—not just go back to where we were before but come out stronger on the other side. The president threw the full resources of the entire United States government at the coronavirus pandemic. The public-private partnerships forged during this crisis demonstrated once again the very best the US has to offer. Factories retooled to produce personal protective equipment (PPE); pharmaceutical companies fast-tracked research and development to create testing to diagnose the virus and speed up research for a cure. As the media continued a narrative that Trump was not doing enough to solve the problem, the president took action and promised us that we were about to embark on the great American comeback.

Though not an easy choice, President Trump's decision to reopen the economy was the right one. He drew from a lifetime of experience in making tough business decisions. He knew that extending the lockdown for any further length of time would put the economy into the same dire position as during the Great Depression. The president had said many times, "The cure can't be worse than the disease." It was time to reopen the world's strongest economy in a smart and methodical way. Predictably, when he did open the country, the Fake News reported that he cared only about his reelection chances and not about how many people would die. Perhaps no other lie it has told about him was more personal and hurtful.

From the first news conference he held during the coronavirus crisis, he said *one* life lost was too many.

One.

Even the president felt the direct impact of the virus on his friends. His longtime friend and business associate Stanley Chera died after contracting Covid-19.

He said it over and over again, yet all you heard and saw from the media was that he cared only about his reelection. When the Chinese foreign minister blamed the US Army for bringing the virus to Wuhan, there was barely a ripple in the liberal press. When Nancy Pelosi called the virus "an inconvenience," not a sound was heard. When Trump called it the Chinese virus, Fake News and the crazy left's army of internet trolls reverted back to their old playbook, calling him xenophobic and racist.

Still, the onslaught by the biased media was taking its toll. The Democrats were using the propaganda the press was spewing to prop up Joe Biden, a broken-down candidate whose best days were far behind him. Though Sleepy Joe is an easy target, coronavirus had put its thumb on the political scale. Without rallies and being out on the campaign trail, the platforms from which the president could hit back the hardest, his success was muted. The left was playing politics at every turn. Even the liberal governor of North Carolina was using the pandemic as a political cudgel to keep the Republican National Convention in Charlotte from taking place.

From a political standpoint, it couldn't get much worse.

Then it did.

———————

At the end of May 2020, with the Covid-19 pandemic in the United States three months old, a white police officer in Minneapolis knelt on a black man's neck until he was dead. That horrific murder was caught on film and reignited the racial divide in America. The president denounced George Floyd's killing strongly and immediately: "All Americans were rightly sickened and revolted by the brutal death of George Floyd. My administration is fully committed that, for George and his family, justice will be served. He will not have died in vain. . . . I will fight to protect you. I am your President of law and order, and an ally of all peaceful protesters."

He then ordered the United States Attorney General William Barr to have the Department of Justice's Civil Rights Division open an investigation into George Floyd's death.

But the evil and shocking incident in Minneapolis would prove to be a flashpoint that ignited riots throughout the country. Peaceful protesters found themselves embedded with domestic terrorists from Antifa and other radical leftist organizations. Mobs marauded through American cities, throwing Covid-19 precautions to the wind, looting stores, and attacking and killing police officers and innocent civilians. Many weak and feckless Democrat mayors and governors did nothing but simply stand by while this American carnage took place. The president responded decisively and boldly to restore order in the streets. Again, his priority was the health and safety of the American people. Still, emboldened by its gains during the Covid-19 crisis, the press unleashed another barrage of incendiary lies in order to help Joe Biden. By the end of May, there were nights when it seemed the country would break in two.

———————————

The Hillary-versus-Trump presidential race was as volatile and unpredictable as we had ever seen, but as it turned out, 2016 now seems tame compared to 2020. The very foundation of political campaigning and the issues impacting the American voter for Joe Biden and Donald Trump have been turned upside down. Just a few short months ago, President Trump was sailing to reelection on the strength of his economy, ending the endless wars, and creating opportunity and prosperity for all Americans. Now we are dealing with the aftermath of a global pandemic, racial tensions not seen since the 1960s, and a group of Republican Never Trumpers hell-bent on destroying the president.

Other than that, everything was going great.

CHAPTER TWO

THE BRAWLERS

Such a beautiful Opening Statement by Corey
Lowandowski! Thank you Corey! @CLcwandowski_
— @realDonaldTrump, September 17, 2019

Before the coronavirus came to our shores, times were good. The outcome of the Mueller investigation crushed what little credibility the media had left. The phony impeachment trial had given Americans little reason to support Nancy Pelosi's vindictive caucus. The economy was booming. The nation was at peace. Unemployment was at historic lows. From our perspective, it seemed pretty simple: the president's reelection chances were better than ever. In one corner, standing on top of the restored American nation, was Donald J. Trump, the heavyweight champion of the world, ready to take on anyone who'd come for his title. In the other corner, half asleep, punch drunk, and propped up by former Obama officials, sat Joe Biden, a creepy old guy whose greatest accomplishment at this point is forming a coherent sentence. Few said it out loud, but the sentiment was pretty clear: this guy didn't have a chance against the champ.

We, too, had just emerged victorious from our own fights. Just like the president, we faced attacks by forces both inside and outside the White House. A day didn't go by, it seemed, without someone taking a shot at us—all that changed was the "where." From the outside, it was the usual suspects we'd battled since the 2016 campaign: the Democrats, their hateful allies on the left, and the Fake News. Though we had gotten good at defending ourselves, they, too, had upped their game. They were smarter, quicker, and as relentless as ever.

The attacks from the inside were more diabolical and harder to see coming. They are more personal, more vicious— and sometimes even physical.

Around noon on February 21, 2018, Corey was sitting in a restaurant near the White House. He was having a cup of coffee with then White House communications director Hope Hicks, whom he had known since the earliest days of the 2016 campaign. Corey was initially supposed to meet Hope at the White House mess located in the basement of the West Wing. That *had* been the plan, at least, until John Kelly stepped in. Earlier that morning, Hope called Corey to let him know that the White House chief of staff had restricted his access to the building.

Kelly, as you might remember, made it his mission to wall the president off from any outside influences, including friends and trusted advisors like us. He was supposed to be "the adult in the room," remember? We all know how that worked out. Last we heard, he was getting booed off the stage at some paid speech in New Jersey.

In the middle of his meeting with Hope, Corey's phone rang. It was Zach Fuentes, John Kelly's deputy, asking Corey if he would be available that afternoon to meet with the chief of staff. After being informed his access to the White House had been restricted, Corey was more than happy to have the chance to speak to Kelly one-on-one.

At 4:30 p.m., Corey was seated at the large conference table at the far side of the chief of staff's office. Before Kelly even entered the room, Corey could feel the hostility. Initially, he thought General Kelly wanted to speak with him about a recently publicized meeting that had taken place in the Oval Office a few months back. At that meeting, which included White House political director Bill Stepien, counselor to the president Kellyanne Conway, 2020 campaign manager Brad Parscale, Hope Hicks, and John Kelly, Corey excoriated the White House's political operation. He told them they were woefully behind where they should be and weren't ready for what was to come in the midterm elections. Corey had rightly predicted that a Democrat wave was about to crash over the House of Representatives. Combined with the mass exodus of Republican retirements from Congress, the caucus would be a shadow of its former self. There was no way it would be able to protect the president, let alone help him advance his "America First" agenda. Once the Republicans lost the House, Corey told them, impeachment wouldn't be far behind.

Though his predictions were spot on, his analysis didn't make him any friends that day. The chief of staff, however, wasn't concerned with that meeting in the Oval Office. What bothered John Kelly was Corey's close relationship with President Trump.

"From now on, if you want to come into the White House, you have to call me first," he said in an exasperated tone.

"That's bullshit," Corey said to himself, but he didn't show his emotions to General Kelly. He mentioned something to the effect of it not being a good use of his time—because it wasn't. With all that the White House chief had to do, it seemed crazy to Corey that John was going to try to be some sort of gatekeeper as well. But Corey knew it would be the wrong move to engage John while he seemed so angry. It wasn't the appropriate time or place . . . for now. Corey tried to ease the tension by reminding the general that they both had the same goal: making sure the president is successful.

"Don't kid yourself," Kelly said, "My goal is to save my country."

If you've ever had a moment when, all at once, your opinion changed, you'll understand how Corey felt. Here was the White House chief of staff telling him that he didn't care if the president of the United States was successful—that he didn't care if the president delivered for the American people or not. Though shocking, Kelly's words weren't all that big of a surprise. Kelly had no qualms about showing his allegiance to the Deep State. According to media reports, after the president fired FBI Director James Comey in May 2017, Kelly called the disgraced head of the FBI and apologized for *the president*! Then he said he would resign from his post as secretary of homeland security if the director wanted him to. The general, it seemed, had different priorities from those of his commander in chief.

If there had been tension in the room before, Kelly's affirmation of indifference pushed it to the next level. Just then, however, Kelly's phone rang; the president wanted to see him in the Oval Office. Tension diffused—for now.

Corey left the office and walked upstairs to visit his old campaign colleague Don McGahn, then the White House counsel, before coming back down to say hello to Dan Scavino, whose office is located just outside the Oval Office. But on his way to see Dan, he noticed that the door to the Oval Office was open. Madeleine Westerhout, at the time the president's personal assistant, told him that the president was free to see him if he would like. As Corey walked in, Kelly began to walk out. As they passed each other in front of the Resolute Desk, Kelly said to Corey under his breath, "Fucking asshole." When Corey asked him what his problem was, Kelly started ranting about Corey "getting rich" off the Trump super PAC.

Getting rich? If anything, Corey was leaking money. He'd already run up a few hundred thousand dollars in fees fighting off the phony Mueller investigation just for being loyal to the president.

The president looked at Kelly and shook his head slowly. "What's wrong with you, John? Corey isn't getting rich," he said, referring to Corey's $10,000-a-month salary from the super PAC. Kelly didn't appreciate that; as a matter of fact, it only enraged him further. The president had defended Corey right in front of him, without even thinking twice. John stormed out of the Oval Office but stalked Corey in the outer Oval, lurking angrily like a petulant child. As Corey and the president began to talk, Madeleine informed the president he had a phone call. It was Christopher Wray, the FBI director.

Corey respectfully excused himself to give the president privacy, and as he stepped out of the Oval Office, he heard Kelly say to someone out of his sight, "When he gets out of there, throw him out of my fucking building."

"Hey, John," Corey said, "last I checked this, isn't *your* building. It's the White House." Tension exploded.

Kelly turned and came running back into the outer Oval Office with his Secret Service protection in tow. He grabbed Corey with both hands and pushed him up against the Oval Office's outside wall. While pushing his hands away, Corey told him to get his fucking hands off of him or he'd call the DC police and have him arrested for assault.

"Or we can just go outside and finish it out there," Corey said. "Up to you, John." Corey grew up in Lowell, Massachusetts. Going "outside" with someone was his default setting.

Corey pointed to Hope's unoccupied office—an alternative option after Kelly's expression said all it needed to in rejecting his offer to step outside. Kelly followed Corey through the open door, and as he closed the door behind him, Corey reminded him that he was in no position to make accusations.

"What are you talking about?" John barked.

"Two words," Corey said. "Rob Porter."

Immediately after taking over the chief of staff role, John Kelly ordered a top-to-bottom review of all staff working in the White House. It had included a review of all security clearances, both those that were pending and those that had already been granted. John Kelly established a rubber-stamp review committee in order to evaluate information coming from the FBI; it treated Trump loyalists one way and Kelly loyalists another.

Above: Team Trump returning to Washington after the Iowa caucuses. *Below:* Dave and Corey visiting a polling place in New Hampshire on primary day.

Above: New Hampshire rally with (right to left) Rep. Mike Johnson, Rep. Mark Meadows, Rep. Matt Gaetz, Rep. Greg Pence, Rep. Tom Emmer, Sen. Lindsey Graham, Rep. Kevin McCarthy, Rep. Steve Scalise. ***Below:*** Aboard Air Force Two.

Above: Aboard Air Force One with President Trump and the Lewandowski family. *Below:* The Bossie family visits with President Trump and the First Lady at the Alabama–LSU football game.

Left: Dave and Corey meet with Israeli Prime Minister Benjamin Netanyahu at his residence in Jerusalem.

Right: Prime Minister Netanyahu shows Dave President Trump's proclamation moving the US Embassy to Jerusalem. *Below:* Netanyahu political team meeting in Israel. Standing: Ryan O'Dwyer and Augie Atencio; seated (left to right): John McLaughlin, Tony Fabrizio, Susie Wiles, Corey, Dave, and Matt Palumbo.

Above: Dave and Corey with Congressman Matt Gaetz at Mar-a-Lago for Call Day. *Below left:* Corey and Dave sign copies of *Let Trump Be Trump* for Republican National Convention staff in Charlotte, NC. *Below right:* President Trump and President Jair Bolsonaro of Brazil attend Kimberly Guilfoyle's birthday party.

Above: Dave attends Judge Brett Kavanaugh's swearing in at the White House.
Below: President Trump and Dave (left) and Corey (right) aboard Air Force One.

Above: Corey testifies before Congress.
Right: Front page of *Washington Times* newspaper signed by President Trump.
Below: Dave attends acquittal speech at White House.

Above left: President Trump golfs with Griffin Bossie as Dave caddies
Above right: President Trump and First Lady Melania Trump arrive at Mount Rushmore for Independence Day celebration. *Below:* Mount Rushmore.

Porter had been the White House staff secretary, a position of enormous importance with almost unlimited access to the president. Just two weeks earlier, the United Kingdom's *Daily Mail* ran interviews with two of his ex-wives, who claimed he had physically abused them. The White House chief of staff had gone forcefully to Porter's defense, calling him a man of true integrity and honor. "I can't say enough good things about him," Kelly said. "I am proud to serve alongside him." Kelly then was forced to state that Porter would slowly transition out of his current role.

However, the next day, the online news outlet the *Intercept* published photos of Colbie Holderness, Porter's first ex-wife, showing her with a black eye. Needless to say, Porter immediately resigned in disgrace.

It would have been bad enough if Kelly didn't know about Porter's past, but because he established the review committee that vetted him, there was no way he couldn't have known. Both of his ex-wives made statements to the FBI. One of his ex-wives had taken out an order of protection in 2010. Even a Google search would have revealed that information. A senior administration official later told the *Atlantic* that Kelly knew about the order.

John Kelly remained chief of staff for almost a full year after the Porter debacle. During that time, he did whatever he could to try to limit our access to the president. He couldn't completely keep us from him, of course, thanks to the help of our friend and White House counselor Johnny DeStefano, who ensured we continued to see the boss. But our limited access still hurt President Trump. We are a part of his team that are his eyes and ears on the outside.

The meeting in Hope's office ended with fewer fireworks than at its start. It was only later that Corey realized John had ripped the buttons off his suit. Had he noticed when he was still outside the Oval Office, the situation might have been worse.

Though Corey did ultimately shake Kelly's hand as a favor to the president, he hasn't forgotten the day John Kelly thought he was above the law. He's also keenly aware that the statute of limitations for the assault hasn't expired.

———————

A little over a year after John Kelly assaulted Corey, Dave had to fight off his own attack. Though it wasn't physical, it was designed to hurt Dave at his core.

In May 2019, an article in the online news outlet *Axios* falsely accused Dave of misleading small donors into thinking that they were giving to President Trump by contributing money to a political arm of Citizens United called The Presidential Coalition (TPC). The piece had the usual anti-Trump suspects' fingerprints all over it. We found out that the Campaign Legal Center, a shadowy left-wing hit squad supported by George Soros, the Southern Poverty Law Center, and Act Blue, had decided to target Dave with a smear campaign.

The story made it seem as though Dave's organization had been created during the Trump presidency and that Donald Trump never heard of it. Neither of those claims was even remotely close to the truth. Dave created The Presidential Coalition in 2005, when George W. Bush had been president, and since then, the organization raised millions of dollars in support of conservative candidates and ideas. For decades, liberals and conservatives alike have raised money for their causes by using the name of the current president. TPC was no different; it was building a war chest while simultaneously spending money tactically to support President Trump's agenda by producing digital ads in battleground states around the country. Dave wasn't trading on the president's name at all, and he had the evidence to prove it—in the president's own voice!

The story was pure Fake News, and the whole thing should have disappeared in a day or two due to Dave's media savvy for killing stories. Unfortunately, there are still people who hold a grudge against us because of our close relationships with the boss—and some of them have the president's ear.

Political power can bring out the worst in people, especially when those people feel threatened. That's what happened to Dave.

Soon after the story broke, the Trump campaign issued a strongly worded statement condemning anyone seeking to profit off the president's name. Though the statement didn't name Dave, the implication was clear: Dave was on the outs.

You have to hand it to whoever orchestrated the hit against Dave: they knew what they were doing. Nothing bothers Donald J. Trump more than the thought of someone making money off his name. But our enemies did it in a way that attacked Dave's integrity, professionalism, and reputation. Though we have been attacked for being partisans, conservatives, and pro-Trump, no one had ever gone after our integrity. It was a first, and we were furious. Too much was at stake to fire back, guns a-blazing, metaphorically speaking—even though that's something we're really, *really* good at. It wasn't the time for counterpunching or blunt force. Righting the situation for Dave would need time and strategy. The long game was the way back.

On a personal level, the hit job was hard to believe. Apart from the president's immediate family, Dave has known President Trump longer than almost anyone working in the White House. He'd been considered for the job of deputy White House chief of staff during the transition and had been publicly reported to be on the shortlist for White House chief of staff to replace John Kelly. No one worked harder for President Trump, and no one was more loyal to his mission. Influential people such as current chief of staff Mark Meadows, Congressman Jim Jordan, and Fox News superstar Sean Hannity all came to Dave's defense. Even with all that help, we both knew that the only way to give the president the truth was to tell him face-to-face. But considering the temperature of the situation, getting a meeting with the president wasn't going to be easy.

As an informal political advisor, Dave had been on the Trump team before just about anyone else. It was Dave, actually, who recommended Corey to Mr. Trump. As you know, Corey would serve as Donald Trump's campaign manager longer than anyone. With Corey guiding the operation, then candidate Trump would win thirty-eight primaries and caucuses and receive more votes than any candidate in the history of the Republican primary process. Some would argue that securing the GOP nomination against sixteen other highly qualified Republicans was a much harder feat than winning the general election. And every step of the way, Corey was talking with Dave on the phone, drawing from his significant political experience.

After Paul Manafort took over the campaign, Dave remained a loyal friend while others turned their backs on Corey. So when Dave joined the 2016 campaign in August as deputy campaign manager alongside Steve Bannon and Kelly-anne Conway, Corey returned the favor by helping out in any way he could. After election day, our friendship became even more substantial. We both played significant roles in the transition; Dave as the deputy executive director and Corey as a trusted advisor. Each of us thought about entering the White House, but in the end we both agreed that as a team, we'd be of greater help to the president working from the outside.

We were right.

The work we've been able to do for President Trump is twofold. First, we try to advise and protect the boss politically. The hundreds of conversations we've had with him about candidates in primaries at the federal and state levels are an example of this. "This guy's great; we think you should endorse him. That guy's horrible; he'll never help you out." We filter through the candidates and encourage him to endorse those who support the Trump agenda and oppose those who won't. Second, we serve as part of his surrogate media operation. We've done literally thousands of media hits, interviews, op-eds, and ad campaigns in support of President Trump. We've also written two other books to tell the true story of the president: *Let Trump Be Trump* and *Trump's Enemies*, both of which are *New York Times* best-sellers. But the point is we're a team, and when you hit one of us, you hit us both.

So Corey knew what he had to do.

Following the attack on Dave in May, the president held a campaign rally in August in New Hampshire. When he touched down in the Granite State just before the rally, he invited Corey and his family, including his mother, to join him on Air Force One. Among other things, the president wanted to talk to Corey about him potentially challenging

Senator Jeanne Shaheen for a Senate seat from New Hampshire. Although the Senate run came up, Corey had something far more important he needed to discuss one-on-one with the president.

He finally got the private moment just before the president went onstage at the rally. The fact that Corey knew him as well as he did before he became the most powerful man in the world allows him to speak to the president uniquely. Though always respectful, he can talk without doing the circular bullshit dance others have to engage in with the president. So when they were both backstage, Corey got right to the point: he told President Trump that he knew for a fact that Dave had done nothing wrong and was being unfairly attacked. He expressed the belief that through his years of friendship and support, Dave had earned the right to speak to the president directly to correct the lie perpetrated months earlier. He encouraged the president to meet with Dave one-on-one.

Within a day, Dave received a call from a staffer asking when he would be available to come into the White House to meet with the president. It was a welcome call and long overdue. For that meeting, he'd go prepared.

Axios reporter Jonathan Swan had written the hit piece on Dave. Swan is considered a dogged reporter with solid sources inside the White House. For these reasons, he is considered a "killer." However, "killers" can lose their status pretty quickly, particularly when the president finds out how false their stories have been.

Swan was no exception.

On August 25, 2019, the day before Dave was scheduled to meet one-on-one with the president in the Oval Office, Swan published a story for *Axios* alleging that the president was considering using nuclear weapons to stop hurricanes. The story was pure fiction and infuriated the president. Dave made copies of the nuclear hurricane article and the one Swan had written about him months earlier. He placed them side by side on the Resolute Desk when he walked into the Oval Office. "Same guy," he said.

That got President Trump's attention.

The next thing he did was play for the president an audio recording he had on his phone. The voice on the tape was Donald Trump's—it had been used for a fund-raising call he recorded back in 2011 for The Presidential Coalition, the very organization that *Axios* had wrongly accused of misusing the president's name.

After listening to the tape, the president leveled Dave with his trademark steely stare. Honed over years of staring down the worst in Manhattan real estate, the look tells whoever's on the receiving end that Donald Trump doesn't like being lied to. At all. Dave knew the look, but for him it took on a different meaning: someone better find a place to hide, and that someone wasn't him.

For *Axios*, there was nowhere to hide. The president called RNC Chairwoman Ronna McDaniel and instructed her that the RNC would never send out another *Axios* story again. Ever. He called Stephanie Grisham, then the White House communications director, into the Oval Office and told her to immediately cut *Axios* off from the White House's information flow. To top it all off, he instructed then chief of staff Mick Mulvaney to inform Swan, an Australian by birth, that he was disinvited from the upcoming White House state dinner for the prime minister of Australia, Scott Morrison.

As far as the president was concerned, *Axios* was dead.

From that meeting on, Dave's relationship with the president has been as strong as or stronger than ever before. Not only did they clear the air, but President Trump was reminded of what he liked about Dave in the first place: he's a fighter, even in the toughest of times. As an exclamation point in putting this unfortunate episode behind them, President Trump tweeted one of The Presidential Coalition's ads demonstrating his gratitude for Dave and the work he and his organizations have done over the years.

New digital ad up in battleground states today highlighting @realDonaldTrump's strong leadership combating the coronavirus Thank you Mr. President.
                                    —@David_Bossie, April 11, 2020

On Easter Sunday, the president retweeted Dave's tweet to his more than 82 million Twitter followers. That day was also the six-year anniversary of the Citizens United Freedom Summit in Manchester, New Hampshire—the event where Dave had first introduced Corey to Mr. Trump and the unofficial kickoff of the 2016 presidential campaign.

Big thanks to @David_Bossie, @Citizens_United & @ AFPhq for hosting me at #NHFreedomSummit. Will be back to the Granite State soon!
                                    —@realDonaldTrump—April 14, 2014

Dave was back on the team, and just in time, too. In the months ahead, the U.S. House of Representatives would move to impeach the president. As the chief investigator in Congress leading up to the Bill Clinton impeachment, Dave knew the inside of that battle as well as anyone. No procedural tricks or committee scheming could get around his knowledge of the process. It would be Corey, however, who almost derailed impeachment before it pulled out of the station.

One of the oldest tricks in the book for federal prosecutors is to exert pressure on a target's inner circle. With enough time and enough pressure, somebody will turn. Those were the very tactics prosecutors used to frame retired general and former national security advisor Michael Flynn. When our friend Rudy Giuliani was the US attorney for the Southern District of New York, he made the tactic an art form, taking down Mafia bosses left and right. Robert Mueller put his own spin on the tactic; instead of jail time, he used lawyer's fees to squeeze those of us close to the president.

Just about everyone in the president's inner circle had to retain counsel. They hired white-collar lawyers who came at premium DC prices. Unlike those targeted inside the White House, whose legal fees were paid by the 2020 campaign, Corey was initially responsible for paying for his own lawyers. By the time he testified, he had racked up nearly $400,000 in billable hours (you'd be amazed how quickly that can happen). But if Mueller thought he could squeeze Corey, he was about to be deeply disappointed.

The House Judiciary Committee, chaired by Democrat congressman Jerrold Nadler of New York, subpoenaed Corey in August 2019. It was supposed to be the first big impeachment hearing of the Mueller Report era. And when we say big, we mean wall-to-wall coverage on every TV channel. Big. There were hundreds of reporters and television cameras outside the Rayburn House Office Building, where the hearing was being held. Fox News had even positioned a camera near the front door. During the pregame show—and that was what it felt like—the crawler that ran under the image read WAITING FOR LEWANDOWSKI'S ARRIVAL.

While those words played on television screens across the country, we were already inside. This latest installment of "professional journalism" gave us a good laugh while we sat waiting in the office of Republican congressman Mike Roger of Alabama down the hall from the committee room in the Rayburn Building. As former Hill staffers, we knew how to navigate Capitol Hill without walking through the front door.

The networks had fallen victim to what many people have done when dealing with Corey: underestimating him. To do so, however, is at your own peril. Congressman Nadler would learn that the hard way. The funniest part was that he thought it would be so easy. Sharp questioning would put Corey on his heels. Nadler's lawyerly ways and years of experience holding public hearings would help him tie together a tight narrative, equally persuasive and damning. Corey, he assumed, would just wither under the hot spotlight or come in unprepared. In short, he was wrong. Completely wrong.

Corey had run through mock questions fired at him from a team of killers for hours. Dave, a former chief investigator for the House of Representatives, led the effort. He was joined by consummate Washington professional Ed Rogers and his colleagues at Barbour Griffith Rogers (BGR). BGR Group mega-fund-raiser Dan Murphy, assorted lawyers who had once served on congressional committees, and our close friend Jason Osborne were also on the team. Every one of them was well versed in the process Corey was about to encounter.

But he didn't just rehearse. In order to refresh his recollection, the research team pulled together every public statement Corey had made in the past.

Corey's outstanding attorney, Peter Chavkin of Mintz Levin, worked with White House counsel to clarify executive privilege and how that privilege applied to Corey. White House counsel also drafted a letter to the committee articulating the White House's rationale for claiming executive privilege. Corey would reference this letter multiple times throughout the hearing—much to Jerry Nadler's chagrin.

The Democrats on the committee—and the liberal left across the country—were counting on what old-time TV fans might call "a Perry Mason moment." They were hoping Corey would collapse under the glare of the klieg lights and the intense questions by Democrat members of the committee.

As though that had a chance of happening.

———————————

After Corey's opening statement, which you can find on page 273 (it's pretty good, if we do say so ourselves), Congressman Nadler began the questioning by recognizing himself. After a long-drawn-out, rambling speech about the unfairness of executive privilege, the congressman finally got specific. Referencing the Mueller Report, he asked Corey if he had met with the president on June 19, 2017, in the Oval Office.

Simple question, right?

Wrong. Corey had watched Robert Mueller testify. He had seen the leeway and privilege that the Democrats had afforded the special counsel. And even with all the coddling, Mueller had begun just about every answer he had given to Congress by asking the page number of the report on which the question was based. He would then start flipping pages until he found the corresponding reference. Anyone who watched the special counsel testify that day could rightly assume that he'd lost a step or two.

"May I have a copy of the report to follow along?" Corey asked.

Given the fact that each member of Congress had a time limit of only five minutes to ask questions, you might be thinking that Corey was trying to run out the clock on Nadler. Although you're entitled to that opinion, we can assure you that stalling was the last thing on his mind. Okay, maybe it wasn't the last thing. It may have been closer to the front of his mind. Okay, fine, he was stalling. It was part of our master plan. If Mueller had been allowed to reference the report, why shouldn't Corey be afforded the same consideration?

"You don't have a copy of the report?" Nadler asked.

"Stop the clock!" yelled congressman David Cicilline, the Trump-hating liberal from Rhode Island.

"You have to start the clock," said Congressman Doug Collins of Georgia.

"He's filibustering!" Nadler complained.

"That's across the hall in the Senate," Congressman Collins shot back. "You can't filibuster here."

A staffer put the report in front of Corey, but it turned out to be the wrong one. By the time they got the right Mueller Report to him, you could have gotten up, made yourself a sandwich, and come to the conclusion that there was no chance of the hearing getting any smoother.

At one point during the hearing, the congressman from California, who had just dropped out of the race for the Democrat nomination for president, began accusing Corey of being ashamed to read quotes from the report out loud. Eric Swalwell is a pompous, arrogant TV hog who is always looking for his fifteen minutes on Maddow.

"President Swalwell, I'm very happy with what I've written, but you're welcome to read it if you'd like."

"Are you ashamed to read it out loud?"

"I'm not ashamed of anything in my life, Congressman. Are you?"

The way we see it, it is all equal: you are afforded the exact same respect you give.

Next up was congressman Hank Johnson of Georgia, a Democrat who feared Guam would tip over if the United States stationed eight thousand soldiers on the island. He likened Corey to "a fish being cleaned with a spoon" before accusing him of being too squeamish to deliver a message from the president to Attorney General Jeff Sessions.

"Why did it take you so long? the congressman pressed. "You chickened out."

"I went on vacation," Corey said. "I took my kids to the beach, Congressman. That was more of a priority."

Sheila Jackson Lee, a Democrat congresswoman from Texas, tried to—well, we're still not entirely sure actually. It was definitely some kind of angry lecture—and it definitely had some kind of point she thought was important. When her time was up, Nadler directed Corey to answer her question. "What question?" Corey asked. "That was a rant." The rest of the Democrats all had their rehearsed lines hoping to rattle him. It did not go well for any of them. Corey was as cool as a spring day in New Hampshire.

As televisions in disappointed liberal households across the country snapped off, the legend of Corey Lewandowski grew in the conservative twitterverse.

Corey was so much in control that he even managed to tease a possible Senate race during his break from testimony. Members of Congress noticed and addressed him about it during the hearing. You can't put a price tag on that kind of advertising.

Afterward, the *New York Post* and other news outlets drew an apt comparison to Oliver "Ollie" North, the lieutenant colonel who had turned the Democrat-controlled joint congressional committee investigating the Iran-contra affair on its head. *The Atlantic* wrote that Corey had tried to make a mockery of the hearings and "Within about five minutes, Lewandowski had accomplished his objective." The CNN headline read, "Lewandowski Stonewalls and Frustrates Democrats in Contentious Capitol Hill hearing." But the biggest rave Corey received was from the boss himself, who live tweeted his thanks from Air Force One.

In one way, the hearing marked the end of the Mueller investigation. Corey would be the first and the last person to testify about anything attached to the phony probe, period. His testimony also ended Congressman Jerrold Nadler's time in the spotlight. Nancy Pelosi yanked the responsibility for the impeachment of the president away from the House Judiciary Committee under Nadler's watch and handed it to Adam

"Full of" Schiff and the House Select Committee on Intelligence. As you may remember, Schiff and his committee didn't fare much better.

———————

With John Kelly now little more than a bad memory, the end of the fake smear campaign against Dave, the collapse of the phony Mueller probe, and Corey's testimony behind him, it felt as though we finally had made it through the worst of the attacks.

We had no idea, of course, that just a few months later, a new virus would begin in Wuhan, China, and spread around the world. All we could see was the campaign trail stretched out in front of us. Now, finally, we were free to do what we do best: help the president of the United States get reelected.

And for the time being, that's exactly what we did.

★

The Democrat Caucus is an unmitigated disaster.
Nothing works, just like they ran the Country. Remember
the 5 Billion Dollar Obamacare Website, that should
have cost 2% of that. The only person that can claim a
very big victory in Iowa last night is "Trump".

—@realDonaldTrump, February 4, 2020

★

CHAPTER THREE

THE CAUCUSES

FEBRUARY 3, 2020, SUPER BOWL SUNDAY

Around 8:00 a.m., Corey got into his black Ford F-150 to head down to Boston's Logan International Airport. He'd made the trip literally hundreds of times since the president first hired him as campaign manager in 2015. On that brisk New England morning, that first meeting in the boss's office atop Trump Tower seemed a lifetime ago. So much had happened since then for Corey, for us, and for the country. Nearly all of it had been good.

From Corey's home in New Hampshire, Logan Airport is about forty-two miles away, a straight shot down Interstate 93. Looking down at his phone before setting off, he checked his boarding pass again. His JetBlue Flight to Washington, DC's, Reagan National Airport was set to depart at 10:14 a.m., right on schedule. Though he had plenty of time, he was still anxious. But today he was even more amped than usual. It was opening day of our favorite season, campaign season. And we were on our way to where, every four years, it all starts: Iowa.

The outstanding senior staff of the Trump campaign had put together what we believed was a juggernaut, perhaps the most well-funded, well-staffed state-of-the-art campaign ever assembled. By that point, all of us on the Trump reelection campaign believed we had built an operation that was unstoppable. Iowa was the chance to kick the tires of the impressive machine and give it its first real test. You can see why Corey was anxious.

Upon arrival at Reagan National, he made his way to the private air terminal to meet up with the rest of the team. By team, we mean the Donald J. Trump campaign leadership team and dozens of surrogates who were all waiting to jump onto a chartered 737 to descend on Iowa. It was a big operation with lots of moving parts, and Corey couldn't wait to see how it turned out.

Later that morning, around 9:15 a.m., Dave walked out of his house in Maryland and jumped into his almost new Chevy Suburban, only the second car he'd had in the last seven years. He had run the old one until it had nearly 150,000 miles on the odometer, and even then he was reluctant to punch the old truck's ticket. For Dave, if something works, you drive it until it dies. Without traffic, Reagan National is a forty-five-minute drive down the Baltimore Washington Parkway. He might have made it to the airport a tick or two quicker than that.

To be clear, it wasn't as though we were sitting home waiting for the Iowa caucuses to start campaigning for the president. Oh, no; we had begun campaigning for the president's reelection as soon as the votes were counted in 2016. Day in, day out, that was our job.

But our eyes have always been on the horizon, looking ahead to the 2020 presidential election. Since June 18, 2019, when President Trump officially launched his reelection campaign in Orlando, Florida, that goal has come into stark focus. In the months before the Iowa trip, we met with the president numerous times to discuss strategy, offer counsel, and receive our marching orders.

In the 2016 campaign, the one thing you could bank on was it was never boring. The 2020 version, however, had already begun putting its younger brother to shame. Those early campaign moments were both historic and absurd.

In December 2019, Dave traveled on Air Force Two with Vice President Pence to Michigan, where the president was doing a rally in Battle Creek. In the early evening before the event at the Kellogg Arena, Dave stood backstage with the president and vice president and watched the Democrat-controlled House of Representatives vote on the bullshit articles of impeachment. It may have been the most outrageous and surreal thing Dave had ever witnessed in his long career in politics. Immediately after the House voted, the president took the stage in the packed arena. He then proceeded to deliver a speech that absolutely blew the roof off the place. He was as good as we'd ever seen him, and on the night of the phony House vote on impeachment nonetheless! Dave always says there's no better game-day player in all of politics than Donald Trump. But his performance at Kellogg was something for the history books.

Watching the president in Michigan, you couldn't help but wonder what universe little Adam Schiff and Nancy Pelosi came from. There has never been a political party more out of touch with hardworking people than the Democrats today. Of course, both of us knew intimately how the Democrats had tried to reverse the results of the 2016 presidential election from the moment Donald Trump was elected. The impeachment, however, was a new low. What frustrated us is that we had known it was coming but couldn't do anything to prevent it. Facts and evidence didn't matter to the Trump-hating Democrats in the House.

Dave arrived at Reagan National first. As he walked into the private hangar at Signature Air, the scene before him made him smile. The space was huge and filled with die-hard Trump supporters and campaign staff. You could feel the energy in the place. As he scanned the crowd, he was struck by the fact that he knew just about everyone there, and so did most Americans.

In addition to being a significant help to the president, our efforts have raised our media profiles considerably, a status that neither of us had before the 2016 campaign. Well, actually, Dave already had a pretty high media profile. Along with his roles on the Trump team, he's also president of the conservative advocacy organization Citizens United. Maybe you've heard of it? Citizens United won a lawsuit in the United States Supreme Court against the Federal Elections Commission that changed the political landscape forever. But since the campaign, some people think we've become political celebrities. It's the Trump Effect. Though being recognized in an airport or asked to sign an autograph (preferably of a copy of *Let Trump Be Trump* or *Trump's Enemies*) is fun, the celebrity thing takes a backseat to our main objective of helping Donald Trump be successful.

Some of the people in the hangar that day have become far more recognizable than us. Many of them, such as congressmen Matt Gaetz, Mark Meadows (whom the president would name White House chief of staff the following month), and Jim Jordan have become household names since Donald Trump was elected. More than just star power, these friends of the president are all smart, media savvy, and dedicated to helping him succeed—as are some of the other VIPs, such as Vice President Pence's brother, Indiana congressman Greg Pence, congressman Rodney Davis of Illinois, our old friend CNN contributor David Urban, and Senior Advisor to the Trump Campaign Katrina Pierson. Commerce Secretary Wilbur Ross and Administrator of the Small Business Administration Jovita Carranza, whom the Senate had confirmed just two days earlier, were among those representing the administration. When you included the senior leadership of the campaign, it was an impressive gathering. One thing was for sure: Iowa was going to feel the campaign's presence.

Corey arrived at the terminal with just enough time to say a quick hello to some of the congressmen and staff before the team headed out to the plane awaiting us for our flight to Iowa.

In October 2019, the campaign had made the strategic decision to put together a large surrogate operation to take Iowa by storm. It would be the first real test of what the 2020 team could pull off and would allow us to work out any potential kinks that might be in the system. But mostly, it was about shock and awe—showing the strength of President Trump's reelection effort by ensuring that he dominated the Iowa caucuses.

Planning for the Iowa operation had been in the works for months, and it showed. From the chartered 737 to assigned

seats and lunch on the plane, to full individual itineraries
including room assignments, credentials, and caucus assignments (drivers and additional staff for each surrogate would
be assigned upon arrival in Iowa), everything had been
thought out to the last detail. It was a pleasure being part of
such a coordinated effort, and we can't thank the campaign
staff enough. We couldn't help but compare it to the 2016
campaign. It wasn't as if we had been unprepared back then,
it's just that we didn't have the same resources. Unlike the
2016 campaign team, the 2020 version had money, an army
of people, and the full support of the Republican National
Committee (RNC).

For at least the first half of the 2016 campaign, we couldn't
get some people in the RNC to answer the phone, let alone
fight from our corner. We ran the 2016 campaign on a self-
funded shoestring. And the number of people we had? Little League teams had more members. We still refer to the
small, tight-knit team as "the island of misfit toys" because,
like Rodney Dangerfield, "We got *no respect.*" Still, we won
against all odds, and that's what mattered. And that's all that
matters in 2020. We never get tired of winning.

The flight to Iowa, at least the first part of it, was like a
college reunion. We traded war stories. Corey told one about
the 2016 Iowa caucuses when in late January that year, in the
freezing cold, candidate Trump ordered him off Trump Force
One with the directive "Go win Iowa for me."

As it turned out, the president finished second in Iowa. It
was, however, one of the last times he'd finish second for the
rest of his meteoric political career. Corey had a lot to do with
that string of successes.

Storytelling time gave way to business. We weren't worried about winning Iowa this time around; we just wanted to win big.

At Des Moines International Airport, chartered buses and a police escort waited to take the massive Trump team to the downtown Marriott, the same hotel where we stayed during the 2016 Donald J. Trump for President campaign. Iowa's weather was a lot more welcoming than four years earlier. During the 2016 caucuses, the state was bracing for a blizzard. Though the big storm never fully materialized, ice and freezing rain made just walking around outside miserable. This time, however, the weather was dry and the temperature was a balmy forty degrees.

At the hotel, we continued seeing faces from the first campaign. In the lobby, we ran into Michael Glassner, a senior campaign advisor of the 2020 campaign. Corey hired Michael back in 2015 on Dave's recommendation. Dave had known Mike since their days working together on the Bob Dole campaign back in 1988, when Mike served as the body man to the then Senate majority leader and World War II hero. Another friend from 2016, Bill Stepien, the future campaign manager, was running a staff-members-only briefing that we attended. Bill served as the president's White House political director and had left to help run the 2020 effort. Prior to the 2016 campaign, Bill served as New Jersey governor Chris Christie's deputy chief of staff in New Jersey; he is a superior political operative. On election night, from the war room, Bill was instrumental in recognizing that candidate Trump had won the state of Florida. Trump's Florida victory marked the beginning of the end of the Clinton Dynasty.

Seeing our old friends reminded us just how incredible the 2016 campaign was. That Donald Trump won the election was a towering feat accomplished by a candidate like no one who had come before. Trump both shocked and changed the political universe forever—and that was only his opening act. No one could have predicted that, as good as he was, candidate Trump would take a back seat to President Trump. How could we have known that the man we crisscrossed the country with on a gold-plated 757 aircraft with TRUMP painted on the outside would transform the presidency and the country forever? The answer is Trump Speed—the intensity with which the president works. "Make America Great Again" wasn't just a slogan, it was a state of mind; it was implicit in everything Donald Trump and his team did. And from what we were seeing so far in Iowa, Trump Speed was pushing past new limits.

Those of us who worked on the 2016 campaign and were now working on the 2020 campaign were given front-row seats to history twice, as well as the awesome responsibility to help Donald J. Trump get reelected for the sake of the country and future generations.

After Stepien finished his presentation, we boarded buses and headed to Smash Park, a local sports bar. Hey, it was Super Bowl Sunday! Once inside, Dave asked Corey and Congressman Gaetz if they wanted a beer and headed to the bar. After ordering three beers, he was given a bill for $18. Usually, gatherings like this have open bars. Free alcohol is the lifeblood of any political campaign. But just as in 2016, 2020 was a dry campaign—or at least one where you had to pay for your own booze. So here was Dave buying a beer at a bash that a billion-dollar campaign was holding. As he handed the bartender his credit card, he couldn't help but smile. The boss is probably getting a kick out of this, he thought.

Both of us are huge football fans. We kept one eye on Patrick Mahomes, the Kansas City Chiefs' star quarterback, who electrified the crowd in Miami while we worked the room. Even if Corey's beloved Patriots didn't fall to Tennessee in the wild-card round and Tom Brady was gunning for a seventh ring, the game would still have taken a backseat to politics. Dave, a Ravens fan, had had the same disappointment of watching his team fall to the Titans earlier in the playoffs. For guys like us, however, the real Super Bowl happens every four years—on the campaign trail.

We chatted with Congressman Kevin Brady from Texas's Eighth District, who as a former chairman of the House Ways and Means Committee shepherded through Donald Trump's historic tax cut. Secretary of the Interior David Bernhardt was with him. Funny enough, security at the door was so tight they almost didn't let the secretary inside. Everyone needed to show credentials issued by the campaign to get in, and the secretary didn't bring them. Dave politely told the security team that the gentleman they were refusing to let in was a member of the president's cabinet—the guy who runs all the national parks. They had enough sense to bend the rules.

We said hello to Kayleigh McEnany, who had traveled to Iowa with her husband, Major League Baseball pitcher Sean Gilmartin, and her newborn baby. She is currently the White House press secretary and previously served as the national spokesperson for the president's campaign. We also saw Laura Nasim, the deputy director of strategic communications and a veteran of the 2016 campaign, where she worked closely with

Dave and Meghan Powers, the director of operations and assistant to Corey back in the day. Laura and Meghan were instrumental in the planning and execution of this incredible trip, right down to the smallest detail. They did an amazing job and are seasoned campaign professionals. When we saw Mahomes raise the Lombardi Trophy, we were happy for him and his Chiefs. Like Donald Trump in 2016, they were the hungrier team, and that got them the win.

Our hunger hadn't faded one bit. We were hungrier than ever and about to show the world what we were capable of.

IOWA CAUCUS DAY

The next morning, Dave and Corey met for coffee in the hotel lobby, where they were joined by Mark Meadows, Jim Jordan, Jerry Falwell, Jr., and his wife, Becki. All are close friends and allies of President Trump. Back in 2016, just a week before the caucuses, Jerry had endorsed then candidate Trump. The endorsement came with a backlash, mostly from a segment of Evangelicals who backed Senator Ted Cruz. To his credit, Jerry never wavered. Instead he doubled down. He and Becki came to Iowa to campaign for Trump. They know a winner when they see one, and Jerry's support of Trump paid off. Evangelicals are thrilled with the president and for good reason. He has happily taken on the role of protector in chief of religious freedom and been an unwavering champion of the sanctity of life. Likewise, no president has ever been more pro-Israel.

What's more, he made sure that the Evangelical cause will be protected for decades by appointing conservative judges at a rate no one has seen before. More on this later, but at the time of this book's publishing, the Senate has confirmed approximately 200 federal judges, including 137 district court judges, 51 appellate judges, and 2 Supreme Court justices. And that's just in the first term of the Trump presidency.

Jerry's endorsement of the president might have been somewhat controversial the first time around, but the Falwells were in Iowa this time not only to make a statement but also to put an exclamation point on it.

At an organized campaign event at the hotel, we sat down for breakfast. Joining us was former Texas governor Rick Perry. A good friend, Rick had just decided to step down as President Trump's secretary of energy. He told us how much he was enjoying his retirement from government service, spending his time with his grandchildren and doing some hunting. In politics, there are moments that can be appreciated only when you look back on them. While sitting with Governor Perry, we were joined by Congresswoman Elise Stefanik from the 21st Congressional District of New York. The congresswoman is one of the rising stars of the Republican Party. You might remember the media attention she garnered during the televised impeachment hearings. The congresswoman and Secretary Perry hit it off right away. When Secretary Perry told her that he was very familiar with her district, he had the table's attention. We wondered how a small-town Texas kid like Governor Perry found himself in upstate New York. It turned out that when Secretary Perry was a pilot in the United States Air Force, he flew C-130 Herculeses and landed at Fort Drum in her district.

At three in the afternoon, the campaign held a press conference as a kick-off to the caucuses. We sat in the front row
of a ballroom packed with Republican Party leaders including Secretary of Housing and Urban Development Ben Carson, then chief of staff Mick Mulvaney, congressmen Kevin
McCarthy and Steve Scalise, Reverend Paula White and
Ralph Reed from the Christian Coalition, and the biggest
celebrity of all, Mike Lindell of MyPillow fame. Mike is
an incredible American success story. From homeless drug
addict to business tycoon, his story of redemption and finding Jesus is truly inspiring. The press conference began as
Brad Parscale, the former 2020 campaign manager, took the
stage. As you might recall, Brad is also a 2016 campaign alum
where he ran its digital media effort. His targeted Facebook
ads ran circles around Hillary Clinton's online presence and
like so many other variables helped to sway the election. An
ex–college basketball player, Brad is six foot eight. With his
beard and buzz cut, he certainly can make an entrance. Brad
and his team worked very closely with both of us along with
Jared Kushner, the president's son-in-law, throughout 2016.
Jared oversaw the messaging as well as other important elements of the campaign and was a significant driver of the
campaign strategy that helped ensure Mr. Trump's election
as president.

Brad was joined by Donald Trump, Jr., Kimberly Guilfoyle, Eric Trump and his wife, Lara. At one point, when Don
Jr. was speaking, a protester approached the stage and began
shouting. It seemed the man didn't think Don Jr.'s father had
done enough to support the state of Israel. The fact that Donald Trump has done more for Israel than perhaps any other

president hadn't seemed to register with the fellow. Some people are never satisfied. Don Jr., a chip off the old block, stayed cool onstage as security escorted the man out after a short scuffle.

Afterward, we were paired with staff volunteers assigned to drive us to our caucus locations. If you've never been to Iowa, there are a whole lot of cornfields between towns. Your caucus site could be forty-five minutes or a three-hour drive away. The campaign had figured out the individual drive times, and we left according to them. We were like strategic bombers in World War II; the strike was coordinated right down to the minute. Though all of the surrogates were handed scripts, we didn't need one. Instead, we relied on our personal relationships with the president. We spoke from the heart about the man who serves as the forty-fifth president of the United States.

Attending an Iowa caucus is a lot like going to a community meeting. People from the neighborhood gather, mostly in schools or other public buildings, listen to surrogates speak on behalf of their candidate, and then cast a vote for their preferred choice. For political animals like Dave and Corey, the Iowa caucuses are a golden opportunity to dig into the campaign at a retail level. Unlike 2016, when there were a number of candidates in the running, 2020 was really a one-man show. Iowa caucusgoers theoretically could have voted for anyone they chose, even someone dead. In reality, we knew that very few Iowa Republicans would vote for anyone other than President Trump. Although the result was a foregone conclusion, the Iowa caucuses still gave us the opportunity to hear what the voters had to say. His one-on-one connection with the voters in the heart of the country was one of the big reasons Donald Trump became president in the first place. We weren't about to turn our backs on them now.

Corey was assigned to a caucus location about forty-five minutes outside Des Moines, while Dave was assigned to Studebaker Elementary School, a site approximately twenty-five minutes away. Neither of us really knew what to expect. It wasn't as though the results were in question, and because of that, we wondered if voters were even going to bother showing up. The campaign, too, was lowballing the expected crowds. We should have known better. The Studebaker school housed two caucus sites, and Dave was told to expect 20 to 25 people in each. But when they pulled up to the school, the parking lot was full. Inside, nearly 150 people were gathered in the school gym, an incredible turnout for a foregone conclusion. And it wasn't as though they were just going through the motions. They greeted Dave enthusiastically and appreciated his short speech and insight into the president.

Corey was met with the same enthusiasm at his site. Iowa voters are like rabid baseball fans; they know the players, their batting averages, and when a team is giving it their all. Corey was given only five minutes to speak, but it was five minutes when he had to be on top of his game. He was. On the way back to the hotel after speaking with Dave, he had only one regret: Dave had already talked to several surrogates to get a bigger read on the evening. He told him that Mark Meadows in particular had been a big hit.

"He called the president during his talk and put him on speakerphone," Dave told him. "The crowd went wild."

"Damn," Corey said, kicking himself. "Why didn't I think of that?" Which was exactly what Dave had said to himself.

———————————

Back at the Marriott that evening, the entire staff gathered in a large ballroom to watch the results, which was sort of like opening a Christmas present you'd already found stashed in your parents' closet. It wasn't a surprise, but it was still good. Actually, it was better than good; it was a wipeout, like the Alabama Crimson Tide playing most any other college football team. For us, Iowa was a test of the team's strength, and we passed with flying colors. The Trump juggernaut was roaring to life. What made the romp even better was watching the Democrat caucuses become a late-night comic's punch line right before our eyes.

The laughs began as soon as the results started coming in. Thinking they were being smart, the Democrat Party once again proved itself arrogant, elitist, and out of touch. They developed a brand-new cell phone app and required caucus chairs throughout the state to report results using it. The app, developed for the party just a few months earlier, was supposed to streamline reporting the results. Sounds good in theory, right? In practice, it was a fiasco. Some chairs never bothered to learn how to use the app. Others received error messages when logging in. Frustrated, some began calling the results in to a central hotline, which jammed almost immediately. Others called state party headquarters but couldn't get through because of the high volume of calls. The Democrats had to revert to counting the ballots by hand and announcing the results piecemeal. By the end of the night,

both South Bend, Indiana, mayor Pete Buttigieg and Vermont
senator Bernie Sanders claimed victory. Joe Biden, who got
swamped, was crying about the results, which he claimed
were tainted. It would be almost a week before the final results
were announced.

There was irony in the Democrats' performance in Iowa.
Here was the party that wants to socialize medicine for the
United States' 330 million people, and it couldn't manage a
caucus with less than 100,000 participants where the hardest
task was counting.

On the flight back to Washington, DC, the team was elated.
We could not have asked for a better outcome in the caucuses,
both ours and theirs. The other senior surrogates and campaign staff—Brad, all the Trump children, a few members of
Congress—had joined us on the plane. Someone came up with
the idea for all of us to wear Make Iowa Great Again hats and
pose for a photo, which we did. The picture received backlash
because the Fake News will do anything if they think it will
get clicks. The false allegation the media made was that Dr.
Ben Carson didn't have a seat toward the front of the plane,
which was why he had been in the aisle for the photograph.
The truth was that Dr. Carson was seated in first class and
had come to the back of the plane for the picture.

In Iowa, President Trump received the highest percentage of the vote of any incumbent president in the history of
the caucuses, and the Democrats were in disarray. While
Corey drifted in and out of sleep on the return flight, Brad
broached the idea with Dave and Bill Stepien of deploying
a similar "shock and awe" strategy in the New Hampshire

primary only a week away. The effort in Iowa had been flaw-less. The team had had months to plan and execute the logistics, the hotel, the travel, the caucus locations—everything. If the Iowa effort was to be repeated only a week later in New Hampshire, it would require a Herculean effort.

On the plane home, Dave began thinking about being with the president a few weeks earlier in Michigan and watching the House vote on impeachment. The thought made him smile. Dave knows politics from the inside as well as anyone who's ever played the game. And he would tell you without hesitation the one axiom that holds true in politics more than anywhere else: you never get mad, you get even.

On February 5, 2020, the Senate was set to vote on the fake articles of impeachment sent over by the House of Representatives. That afternoon, Corey and Dave took a car from their offices on Capitol Hill to the US Capitol. Dave texted several senators the day before to inquire about getting tickets to the Senate gallery for the historic vote. Each senator received only three tickets, so they were hard to get. Luckily, Dave has a lot of senators' phone numbers in his phone. It was a day for the history books, and Dave and Corey wanted to be there in person. Only twice before had the Senate voted on impeachment articles against a president.

We sat high above the Senate floor and watched as the one hundred senators filed in and took their seats behind the very desks that had once been the province of John Quincy Adams, Daniel Webster, and John F. Kennedy, to name a few. The chief justice of the United States Supreme Court, John Roberts, gaveled the assembly to order. The two Articles of Impeachment were for abuse of power and obstruction of Congress. One by one, the clerk called the senators by name in alphabetical order, and one by one, they rose from their desks and voiced their votes. On news broadcasts across the country, columns totaling the yeas and nays began to fill. With each vote, it became more evident that President Trump would be acquitted on both counts by a considerable majority. We'd sat above the Democrat section so we could watch the Republicans vote. When it was Mitt Romney's turn to cast his vote, Corey turned to Sergio Gor, Senator Rand Paul's then deputy chief of staff, and in his best radio announcer's voice, said, "And here's Pierre Delecto." Sergio laughed. Romney's made-up Twitter handle, which rates only second to Anthony Weiner's Carlos Danger, never fails to get a laugh. On the floor, Romney wanted it both ways; he voted guilty on the first article and not guilty on the second, making him the first senator in American history to vote to impeach a president of his own party.

Romney aside, when Chief Justice Roberts uttered the words "Not guilty" on both articles, we wanted to jump out of our seats. It wasn't because we were surprised; our reaction was one of relief that we hoped the witch hunt was finally over. We knew that since election day 2016, the goal of the Democrats was to impeach this president. Though we couldn't stand and cheer as did millions of Americans who were watching their TVs (the hallowed chamber would not stand for such a celebration), no one could stop us from smiling. The media reported on our attendance and said that we had given each other a fist pump after the not guilty announcement was read. After three years of an unprecedented attack against the president, the final shackles had come off Donald J. Trump. We had witnessed one of America's great moments. For Democrats, however, the acquittal was a nightmare come true. And, the best part was, they hadn't seen anything yet.

Now things were really going to get interesting.

★

I will be there in two weeks, The Southern White House!
— @realDonaldTrump, December 12, 2019

★

CHAPTER FOUR

CALL DAY AT MAR-A-LAGO

FEBRUARY 7, 2020

During the 2016 campaign, Corey called Mar-a-Lago home for the better part of two and a half months. He was gone so long that when he returned to the campaign office in the Trump Tower in March, the campaign staff had made a sign that read WELCOME BACK! As winter campaign headquarters go, the president's Palm Beach club isn't a big sacrifice. Some nights, Corey stayed in a 1,000-square-foot oceanfront suite in Mr. Trump's adjoining beach club. Every other campaign staffer in the country wished they could have the privilege to work from such an amazing facility. Some of the highlights of his extended stay included meeting Patriots coach Bill Belichick, a football hero of his, and hearing the band Chicago play an impromptu set for the guests in the club that evening.

One of his best memories of that time is when he got to drive the car of his dreams.

He had just returned from a campaign trip with Mr. Trump. When the SUV pulled into the mansion, there was a brand-new red Ferrari parked in the driveway. Corey's face lit up like a Christmas tree when he saw the Ferrari, and he said, "What a beautiful car!"

"It's mine, want to take it for a ride?" Mr. Trump asked.

The next day, like most Sunday mornings, the boss would watch the Sunday shows or enjoy some time with friends. Meanwhile, the campaign staff would try and catch up on all the work that piled up during the previous week. But that Sunday, Corey walked over to the valet who was waiting for him with a set of keys. Instead of sitting in front of his computer, he spent the next couple of hours tooling around Palm Beach and the roads along the ocean in the red Ferrari 458 Italia that had a whopping 980 miles on it. Nothing against the Ford Motor Company, but the sleek Italian beauty beat his F-150 pickup truck by a mile or ten.

By early February 2020, the campaign was firing on all cylinders—just like the 458. We looked solid in just about every poll and were amassing an unprecedented war chest. From just online donations, the GOP had raised nearly $120 million during the impeachment hearings alone, about $1 million a day! It had also registered 1 million new donors. That's how much the American people believed Adam "shifty" Schiff.

The relationship between the RNC and the Trump 2020 campaign is a lot different from what it was in 2016. Prior to Mr. Trump accepting the nomination in 2016, there was limited interaction. In this cycle, however, the joint fund-raising committee has raised, as of this writing, over $750 million with $300 million cash on hand for President Trump's 2020

run for reelection. We don't call it the "billion-dollar campaign" for nothing. The RNC is also sharing data and other
resources with the campaign in an unparalleled manor. The
organization that literally wouldn't answer our calls before
the 2016 convention is now working shoulder to shoulder with
the campaign to get the president reelected.

The combined RNC-Trump campaign data collection,
voter registration, and on-line advertising is the most state-
of-the-art operation the political world has ever seen. The
army of surrogates, most of whom are seasoned, recognizable
media pros, are set to help overwhelm any lies and falsehoods
the opposing campaign tries to push. Some of them you'll recognize as staff from 2016, such as current senior advisor Jason
Miller. They've gone into battle before—and won. And this
time, our candidate is a president that has made good on the
promises he made on the 2016 campaign trail.

With money and support for the president flowing in, the
campaign was doing all it could to keep the momentum—and
we were a big part of that.

On February 6, 2020, Corey left his offices on Capitol Hill and
jumped into an Uber headed for Reagan National Airport to
catch the two o'clock flight to Palm Beach International (PBI)
airport. Dave headed to the airport with Congressman Matt
Gaetz directly after an event at the White House. President
Trump had invited some of his closest supporters to the East
Room to thank them for their support during the impeachment hearings. At times, Reagan International is a political junkie's paradise. There are so many boldfaced political

names walking around the airport, it's like being in the lobby of the Trump International Hotel in DC during an open-bar event.

As soon as he walked into the airport, Corey ran into Sergio Gor, who was also on his way down to Mar-a-Lago. While they were sitting at an airport bar waiting for Dave, Reince Priebus, a former White House chief of staff, walked by. Reince was on his way to give a speech in Florida and stopped to say hello. By the time Dave showed up with Congressman Gaetz, Senator Lindsey Graham, RNC chief of staff Richard Walters, and many other political heavyweights had already gathered in the boarding area. The next day, Friday, February 7, 2020, was "Call Day," a huge fund-raising event hosted by the Trump Victory Finance Committee held at the Winter White House.

Once we landed in Palm Beach, we drove straight to Mar-a-Lago. Though Call Day, the main event of the weekend, wasn't until Friday, there were a couple of other fund-raisers at the club that we had been invited to. The first was a cocktail reception and dinner Thursday evening for St. Jude Children's Research Hospital in Memphis, Tennessee. Eric and Lara Trump have been big supporters of St. Jude for many years and have raised millions of dollars for the hospital. The next morning, we attended fund-raiser number two, also at Mar-a-Lago, this one for Senator Rand Paul. Senator Paul was gracious enough to ask both of us to say a few words.

Following the breakfast for Senator Paul, we headed to the club's giant ballroom, where we were greeted by our old friend Keith Schiller, who served as Mr. Trump's bodyguard for almost two decades. Keith is truly one of the good ones. You know exactly where you stand with him at all times. He was always the person we turned to when we had a question about Mr. Trump during the campaign.

The ballroom was quite a sight: there were hundreds of people working the phones, calling friends and family, coworkers and business partners with the goal of helping Donald Trump get reelected. In the front of the room there was a long table where members of the Trump family sat and fielded calls. There were two giant screens set up behind them, tracking all the contributions that were pledged and the people who helped secure the gifts. Boy, things had come a long way!

For those of you who are wondering, the Trump Victory Finance Committee is composed of Donald J. Trump for President, Inc. ("the campaign"), the Republican National Committee, and the official Republican state party committees in various states. Though the inner workings of the committee get pretty involved, the easiest way to describe it is like this: it's a vehicle for donors to fund both the RNC and the Trump campaign with one check.

The indefatigable Kimberly Guilfoyle, whom many of you will remember from Fox News' The Five, chairs the Trump Victory Committee. As far as organizers go, Kimberly has to be one of the best. Liberals constantly underestimate Kimberly, thinking that she's simply an ex–Fox News host or got her position because she's the girlfriend of the president's son. What they don't know is that she is so proficient at tae kwon do that she once kicked a heavy bag right out of its mount. She graduated from the University of California, Davis, magna cum laude, studied law at Trinity College in Dublin, Ireland, and earned a Juris Doctor degree from the University of San Francisco School of Law. After she passed the bar, she worked as a deputy district attorney for Gil Garcetti during the O. J. Simpson trial and later as a no-nonsense assistant district attorney in San Francisco.

In other words, she's an absolute killer.

Kimberly didn't just set up, and perfectly execute, national Call Day—she also manages the entire bundler program. "Bundlers," as we call them, are people who commit to raising large sums of money for the president's campaign. In 1999, George W. Bush called the bundlers, each of whom pledged to raise $100,000 for him, "the pioneers." Hillary called hers "the HillRaisers." The Trump Victory Finance Committee didn't waste time trying to come up with cute names; raising money was the more important objective. Instead, each of our bundlers was assigned a number. Corey's is 007. 007 was also his Secret Service security pin number when he ran the presidential campaign back in 2016. We're not making this up.

Raising funds for the president wasn't the hardest job we've ever had, but we still had pretty high expectations for ourselves. The process is pretty straightforward: the bundlers call people they know, known supporters of the president mostly, and ask them to donate. In that regard, fund-raising for President Trump is a cinch. However, there are still some instances when the bundler has to employ a little finesse. For example, Tom Hicks runs a private equity investment fund and is a big supporter of the president. His son Tommy Hicks, Jr., a great pal of ours and a veteran of the 2016 campaign, serves as the cochair of the Republican National Committee.

He, too, was bundling with us on Call Day. When Dave suggested that he call his father, Tommy was reluctant and asked Dave to do it instead. No red-blooded American likes to call their father for money—even money for the Trump campaign—especially when it's your father's birthday. Dave had just recently had lunch with Tom Sr., so he jumped in and dialed the number. When Tom Hicks, Sr., answered the phone, Dave said, "First off, Happy Birthday, I hope you're having a good day. But I'm also calling because Tommy Jr. didn't want to ask you for money." Tom Sr. got a good laugh out of that one. He wrote a $150,000 check.

In the case of certain big donors, Don Jr., Kimberly, Eric, or Lara jumped on the phone to thank them personally, which helped a lot. But even when it was just us on the phone with potential donors, they were thrilled. By the end of the day, Corey had raised somewhere around $100,000, while Dave secured around $350,000, including Tom Hicks's donation—in total, nearly a half a million dollars from the dynamic duo! Not bad for a couple hours' work.

Call Day was an unmitigated success. By day's end, the committee had raised north of $35 million—more than we had spent during the first fifteen primaries in 2016. It was the most massive one-day total for political fund-raising ever. This was Trump 2020 operating at full force.

That afternoon, after we finished our calls, we walked from the grand Palm Beach mansion to an awaiting vehicle and headed to the airport. We each had our own memories of the club, Dave's going back years. But it was after he had been named deputy executive director of the presidential transition team that he spent the most time there. He reminded Corey of the time when the transition team stayed at Mar-a-Lago longer than we had packed for. One day when Dave had been running out of clothes, he went down to the gift shop, selected a polo shirt, and then signed for it with the room number of Dan Scavino, one of the originals. Dan's room was Dave's version of "the Underhill account." If you've seen the Chevy Chase movie *Fletch*, you know what we're talking about.

Still, as the failed presidential candidate Senator John Edwards, a Democrat from North Carolina, once said, "The trouble with nostalgia is that you tend to remember what you liked . . . and you forget what you didn't." Looking back at our time at Mar-a-Lago and the 2016 campaign is fun, and there certainly won't ever be anything like it again, in politics or anywhere else, but helping the president win in 2020 is even better. If we had had any doubt—and we didn't—Call Day proved that we were part of a reelection campaign that was a juggernaut. There truly was no time like the present.

That afternoon, we did what we always do: packed our bags and hit the road. We were lucky enough to hitch a ride back to Washington on a private plane. One of the perks of our work is getting to know people who have bank accounts slightly larger than ours. When we say slightly, we mean that the decimal point is about three digits in the opposite direction. The flight got us into Washington two hours earlier than we would have arrived if we had taken the commercial flight we booked. And it was a good thing we saved some time; Corey had an invite to the Republican Governors Association dinner, where the president was going to speak, and he had to drop off his luggage and get dressed for the event. He made it to the Andrew W. Mellon Auditorium just in time.

SHOUT OUT

A beautifully ornate room built in the 1930s and owned by the United States government, the Mellon Auditorium on Constitution Avenue in DC has plenty of history. A few of the events that occurred there, however, aren't among President Trump's favorite topics. It was at the Mellon that President Franklin Delano Roosevelt signed the North Atlantic Treaty in 1949. The Mellon was also the site of President Bill Clinton's signing of the North American Free Trade Agreement into law. But NATO and NAFTA were far from the president's mind that night. That night was all about the might of the Republican Party at the state level. Governors and their significant others, family, and friends filled the room to capacity. Though they didn't know it, each of the governors would soon find their legacies tied to how they handled the pandemic of the century.

During the cocktail hour, Corey had the chance to introduce Scotty Smiley to several of the governors, including Nebraska governor Pete Ricketts. Governor Ricketts is of the famed Ricketts family, which owns the Chicago Cubs, among other things. He has been a great supporter of the president dating all the way back to when candidate Trump first made a trip to Nebraska during the 2016 primaries.

In 2005 in Iraq, Scotty lost one eye and his sight in the other when an insurgent detonated a bomb in the trunk of a car. Barely clinging to life, army personnel transported him to Walter Reed National Military Medical Center. There they told him he would never see again. Scotty and his wife, Tiffany, turned to God for help.

Miraculously, he recovered from his life-threatening wounds at Walter Reed. When an army medical review board deemed him fit, he became the first blind active-duty officer to serve in the US Army. A graduate of West Point with a master's in business from Duke University, he is an American hero and the embodiment of American perseverance.

Corey also ran into our old friend from the 2016 campaign South Carolina governor Henry McMaster. Lieutenant governor at the time, Henry was the first and only statewide officeholder to endorse Mr. Trump before the South Carolina primary. Henry got on board the Trump Train from the beginning and has been a big help ever since.

The president was in an even more cheerful mood than usual when he took the stage, and for good reason: he was coming off a week of victories. Two days earlier, the United States Senate acquitted him of the phony impeachment articles, ending the Democrat witch hunt once and for all. Three days earlier, he delivered a State of the Union address for the ages that Speaker Pelosi didn't appreciate very much. With each line of his speech, the list of his accomplishments grew to an extraordinary record of achievement. At the end of each line, the Republicans' side of the chamber exploded in applause as the Democrats sat with arms crossed and grim faces. Jerry Nadler looked just as he had when Corey testified in front of his committee—completely lost. With each line, the prospect of four more years, a chant that greeted the president when he entered the House chamber that night, grew more and more probable.

Trump being Trump, however, the State of the Union address was also a show. He made a young black girl's dream come true by awarding her a scholarship to a school she coveted.

He arranged for a live reunion of an active-duty soldier and his wife. The moment, however, that made the heads of millions of liberals explode—and maybe the one that drove House speaker Nancy Pelosi to rip up her copy of the speech on live TV—was when the first lady draped conservative radio icon Rush Limbaugh with the Medal of Freedom. Talk about being triggered.

Ka-boom!

At the RGA dinner, Corey had a ringside seat at the head table directly in front of the podium where the president was speaking. As the president began his remarks, he noticed our old friend and White House staffer Johnny McEntee standing in the wings. Johnny, an ex–Division I quarterback at the University of Connecticut, had started as a volunteer on the 2016 campaign but was so enthusiastic and dedicated that we made him an official part of the campaign team. When President Trump assembled his White House staff, he named Johnny as his body man. When John Kelly was named White House chief of staff, he fired Johnny. Kelly's destructive time in the White House was remarkable, but the firing of Johnny was one of the lowest moves he made. Kelly was looking for a reason to purge the White House of Trump loyalists and used a bullshit accusation against Johnny to get rid of him. Firing him also showed just how out of touch Kelly was. The president loves Johnny, and Johnny is as loyal to the president as you can be. Still, what goes around comes around! Politics has a way of settling scores, and seeing Johnny again at the president's side while General Kelly is out pretending he's still relevant, made Corey smile. Johnny was back where he belonged, and he was a sight for sore eyes.

The big moment of the night, however, came during the president's speech. Right in the middle of it, he saw Corey in the audience and stopped. "Cor-ree!" he said, genuinely surprised and happy. "My Corey."

Now, in telling you this story, we realize we're taking a risk of sounding boastful or self-important. But the point is, for the president of the United States, during a speech to a room filled with Republican governors, major donors, and supporters, to call out a political operative such as Corey is like the Pope calling you a good Catholic. You can't fold up the moment and put it into your pocket, but everybody in the room knows you've been blessed by him.

When the president finished his remarks, Corey jumped the rope (with the permission of the Secret Service, of course) and went backstage to spend a few minutes with the boss before he left. The president asked how the fund-raising at Mar-a-Lago had gone earlier in the day and was thrilled when Corey told him it was a home run, with huge numbers. He then invited Corey to fly with him to New Hampshire on Air Force One the following Monday. The campaign had scheduled a rally ahead of Tuesday's primary. As much as Corey wanted to go, he had to graciously decline, as he'd planned to spend some time with his family over the weekend. Road warriors like us have to grab opportunities when they arise. But he also wanted to have a few days to make sure everything was buttoned up for the primary—the venues, the events, the right people in the right places, and so on. For Corey, politics in New Hampshire is a home game.

We weren't about to take any chances.

CHAPTER FIVE

HOME GAME

95% Approval Rating in the Republican Party, a
Record! 53% overall (plus add 9 points?). Corrupt
Democrat politicians have brought me to highest
polling numbers ever with the Impeachment Hoax.
Thank you Nancy!

—@realDonaldTrump, February 10, 2020

Historians will say it all began in New Hampshire. Back in April 2014, Dave and J. T. Mastranadi, Citizens United's political director, came up with a concept of hosting an event for presidential hopefuls in the early primary states. They called it the Freedom Summit Series and invited a star-studded roster of speakers to appear. The exclusive list included senators Rand Paul, Ted Cruz, Arkansas governor Mike Huckabee, House speaker Newt Gingrich—oh, and Donald Trump. Not that he was an afterthought, mind you, but back then, he hadn't fully decided whether or not he was going to run for president in 2016. Hell, even if he had, no one would have taken him seriously. Dave had been an informal political advisor to the future president for years. He knew well Donald Trump's history of dipping a toe in the presidential waters, only to pull it out just as quickly. Still, this time around, something seemed different. In 2013, Dave had asked then pollster Kellyanne Conway to conduct a poll of Mr. Trump's chances in the New York State gubernatorial race against Andrew Cuomo. No one was surprised that the boss's name recognition numbers were off the charts. What did surprise them, however, was the response to the question Mr. Trump decided to add at the last moment: "Would you rather see Donald J. Trump run for governor or President of the United States?"

The New Hampshire Freedom Summit also marked the first time Corey and Dave worked together. That connection happened like this: In the early 2000s, Corey worked for New Hampshire Republican senator Bob Smith together with Jeff Marschner. Several years later, Jeff went to work for Dave at Citizens United. When Dave went looking for someone who knew the political landscape in New Hampshire, Jeff recommended Corey. Up until then, Dave knew Corey by reputation only. He quickly found out that he came as advertised.

The weather had cooperated for the day of the Freedom Summit. It was crisp and clear, one that most people would have spent working in their yards or playing with their kids, not attending a political event. However, the event drew a packed house—over a thousand people squeezed into a conference room in the Courtyard by Marriott. Back then, senators Paul and Ted Cruz were front-runners, and both had followers in the crowd. They both gave rousing speeches. But the feeling in the room changed when Mr. Trump took the stage to Frank Sinatra's version of "New York, New York."

He talked well past his allotted time (no surprise there), but no one cared. The room was filled with limited-government conservatives and libertarians, not precisely a brash New York City billionaire's type of crowd. Still, he had them eating out of the palm of his hand. He talked about building a wall on our southern border, and the crowd erupted in applause. He spoke of the economy, trade, and everything else that he'd promise to fight for during his campaign (and then keep those promises as the forty-fifth president of the United States). With each pledge, the audience's applause grew louder.

Anyone who ever saw him on *The Apprentice*, which means just about everyone alive, knows how good Donald Trump was in front of a camera. But the connection he had with a live audience was astounding. One minute he had them laughing; the next, they were ready to storm the Capitol.

But it wasn't his oratorical skills, abundant as they were, that made us believe we were witnessing something special. No, that epiphany came by watching the crowd. Just about everyone in the audience was holding up a cell phone, capturing his speech on video. We'd seen that before, but not to the extent we witnessed that day. His words became electric, both figuratively and literally. Every one of those videos was going to be posted on Facebook or seen by friends and family. His reach was exponential—limitless, actually. Though Mr. Trump wouldn't ride his golden escalator and officially announce his candidacy until more than a year later, it was at that moment in New Hampshire that we saw a potential candidate like none we'd ever seen before.

It might also have been the first time he used the phrase "Make America Great Again" in public. It was certainly the first time those words began to resonate with a crowd. With his speech that day, he was truly testing the waters for some of the language he would use to incredible effect on the campaign trail. Along with "Make America Great Again," he gauged the audience's reaction to lines like "Not free trade, smart trade" and "I would build a border like nobody's seen before." Of his many talents as a candidate, his ability to have his finger on the pulse of the crowd at his speeches and rallies to obtain a real-time feel for Americans' opinions on issues is one of the least talked about.

Following his speech, Mr. Trump accompanied Dave over to Radio Row. There Dave reintroduced him to Stephen K. Bannon. Mr. Trump proceeded to conduct a lengthy radio interview with Steve, who had already become a big fan of the future president, on a wide range of topics. Mr. Trump also conducted an on-camera interview with "Campaign" Carl Cameron of Fox News. Speaking with the media after an event or speech was another strategy candidate Trump began to hone in New Hampshire. While Hillary couldn't wait to get back into her SUV after a political stop, Mr. Trump would take questions from the media for an extended length of time. Though a political neophyte, he inherently knew how to use his time in the most advantageous way we'd ever seen. Fresh off a rally and having read the crowd's reaction, he knew what message his base wanted to hear. Speaking with the press after an event gave him the opportunity to get that message out on the airwaves nearly instantaneously. It was really genius.

A little less than six years later, we waited for the president's arrival at Signature Aviation, a private air terminal at Manchester-Boston Regional Airport. It was the same terminal where he landed his Sikorsky S-76 the day of the Freedom Summit. Dave thought back to how gracious Mr. Trump had been to his son, Griffin. By the time he was three, Griffin had gone through several operations on his heart and brain. Once Mr. Trump found out about Griffin's health issues, he went out of his way to help as much as he could. Griffin's recovery was nothing short of miraculous, and now he's a fine, healthy seventeen-year-old with a single-digit golf handicap. One of his ambitions was to play a round of golf with the president of the United States. A little later in the book, we'll tell you how he reached that goal. It's quite a story.

After Mr. Trump had given his speech at the Freedom Summit, he asked Griffin, Dave's daughter Lily, and Corey's daughter, Abigail, if they wanted to take a ride in his helicopter. Dave thought he was kidding at first, but the next thing they knew there they were, Dave, Griffin, Lily, and Dean Palumbo, the son of our friend Matt (Abigail was a little young and didn't want to go), strapped into the leather seats and holding on to the 24-karat gold–plated fixtures in the helicopter. Most people never get to see the president's soft side and big heart. All they see is the no-nonsense, hard-hitting commander in chief.

For those of you who don't know, here's a little insight: no one cares more for children, or for less fortunate people, than President Trump. Remember that the next time you see some liberal assassin on MSNBC making him out to be a monster. If you knew President Trump as we do, you would know that he has a special place in his heart for all children, no matter where they come from.

From where we stood at the airport, we could see Air Force One turn in to its final descent. It was a clear night, and in the distance, the majestic jet looked like an eagle circling its prey. Waiting with us for the president's arrival were the great Al Baldasaro and Lou Gargiulo, two of the campaign's New Hampshire cochairs. Soon Stephen Stepanek, the New Hampshire state Republican Party chairman, along with New Hampshire governor Chris Sununu, joined the welcoming committee. Dave reminisced with the governor about working with his dad and brother. John H. Sununu, as you might remember, was a three-term governor of New Hampshire and later served as President George H. W. Bush's White House chief of staff. His son and Chris's brother John E. Sununu is a former congressman and senator from New Hampshire. Dave's relationship with Senator Sununu goes back to his time in Congress and the House's investigation into Bill Clinton. Dave reminded the governor about an encounter he once had with his brother when he was a congressman. John E. Sununu was wearing a New Hampshire–themed tie. As Dave's father was born and raised in North Woodstock, New Hampshire, in the White Mountains, the tie piqued his interest. He asked the congressman where he had gotten it. "My dad would love it," he'd said.

The congressman removed his brand-new tie and handed it to Dave, who has never forgotten the kind gesture.

Having the most famous aircraft in the world taxi up so close to you that you can almost reach out and touch it—at least if you were sixty-three feet tall—is also an unforgettable experience. Both of us had flown with President Trump on Air

Force One on numerous occasions but had never been part of a welcoming committee. First off, the plane carried an all-star team of Trump allies on the Hill: House minority leader Kevin McCarthy, Senator Lindsey Graham, Congressman Matt Gaetz, Congressman Mike Johnson of Louisiana, soon-to-be White House chief of staff Mark Meadows, and House minority whip Steve Scalise. It was a thrilling moment that was nearly ruined by a self-important volunteer staffer.

Just prior to the airplane's arrival, a guy we'd never seen before was arranging people and shouting orders. We had no problem with his enthusiasm, and we didn't mind when he directed his orders at us—we're not royalty, not by a long shot. Corey politely explained that Dave would be jumping into the staff car of the presidential motorcade to the event.

By the time the plane landed and the wheels were chocked, the same staffer was barking orders at members of Congress to hurry up and get into the motorcade as to not delay the president's departure to the arena. Protocol and security demand expediency when deplaning from Air Force One. But this guy was way over the top—even for two guys like us who like to make sure things run on time. At one point, he started yelling at congressman Steve Scalise, who he thought was holding up the motorcade because he wasn't moving fast enough to get into his assigned vehicle. For anyone who doesn't remember, congressman Scalise was shot while practicing for the annual congressional charity baseball game by a deranged lunatic supporter of Bernie Sanders. The congressman barely survived his injuries. He's undergone numerous operations just to allow him to walk again, and here's this staffer telling him to run. If the president had known that the guy had spoken to the congressman that way, he'd have blown a gasket and fired him on the spot.

This is what happens when a presidential campaign gets big: people who fill minor roles become self-important and arrogant. The reason they got the job in the first place was the vetting process gets thin and decisions are made too quickly to fill positions. No one takes the time to find out if the person they're hiring is going to represent the president professionally. Judging by the way that guy talked to Congressman Scalise, we could only imagine how he would treat someone who wasn't as heroic. To run a good presidential campaign, you have to make sure that everyone knows, from the lowest staffer to the campaign manager, that they are representing the candidate. That means treating everyone you meet with dignity and respect.

Part of our self-described job description is rooting out the bad apples both in the administration and on the campaign. We've had a lot of practice, and most of it has involved people a lot more dangerous to the president and the administration than low-level campaign staffers. We began sharpening this skill back during the presidential transition. The number of people who've appeared out of nowhere and claimed they had been with the president all along was staggering. Jumping on the bandwagon after the hard stuff is over is fantastic work if you can get it. Some of the people were harmless, but some weren't. Never Trumpers faked their way into prominent positions within the administration. We wrote about this extensively in our first two books, *Let Trump Be Trump* and *Trump's Enemies*. Like a growing cancer, they sought only to sabotage the president at every turn by leaking information to the press, blatantly disobeying orders, and conspiring with other traitors. The phony Mueller scam, a witch hunt that totally exonerated the president, was filled with them.

You remember the names: Associate Deputy Attorney General Bruce Ohr and his wife, Nellie Ohr. Nellie Ohr worked along disgraced former MI6 operative Christopher Steele. It was she who started the Russia probe fiction by passing along Steele's phony dossier to her husband inside the Department of Justice. Then there was FBI rat Andrew McCabe and US attorney Jessie Liu, who refused to prosecute him. Then came the Ukraine letter and the articles of impeachment, and more reptiles crawled from the Swamp: Colonel Alexander Vindman, supposed Ukraine whistle-blower Eric Ciaramella, and Inspector General of the Intelligence Community Michael Atkinson.

And then there was David Holmes.

You might remember Holmes from the impeachment hearings. He was the US diplomat in Ukraine who supposedly overheard both sides of a telephone conversation between the president and Ambassador Gordon Sondland. In front of the House Judiciary Committee, Holmes testified that the president inquired about Ukrainian president Volodymyr Zelensky's intentions to investigate the business dealings of Hunter Biden. That feat of superhearing had been accomplished even though the ambassador's phone was *not* on speaker and Holmes was sitting at least four feet away from him.

One of Citizens United's core missions is filing Freedom of Information Act requests to obtain documents hidden deep in the administrative state. They often go to court when government agencies deny their request. Over the past few years, CU has sued the Department of State for documents attached to the Steele dossier and Fusion GPS. Through FOIA, Dave's organization uncovered a connection between alleged whistle-blower Eric Ciaramella and George Soros's Open Society Foundations going back many months.

It was also through a FOIA request that CU would uncover information pointing to David Holmes being even further involved in the Deep State than his fantastical testimony indicated. They found the information in a trove of documents from the National Security Council that contained an email chain between well-known Trump haters inside the NSC and State Department. One of the people included in the chain was Stephanie Holmes, David Holmes's wife; while her husband was testifying before Congress, pretending to be a patriot, his wife was in direct contact with the deepest part of the Deep State.

On January 30, 2020, soon after Dave's organization found the emails, we had a meeting with the president in the Oval Office. When Dave told him what he had come across and then handed him the proof, the president summoned his White House counsel, Pat Cipollone, and National Security Advisor Robert O'Brien. Cipollone was not in the building and therefore was unable to join us. O'Brien and Mick Mulvaney, who had joined us in the meeting, were unaware of the documents. The president ordered O'Brien and Mulvaney to get to the bottom of it by working with the White House counsel. Though we don't know for sure, we'd guess that the investigation is ongoing with more to be revealed about David Holmes.

———

It was just a short eight-minute drive to the rally that was held that night at the Southern New Hampshire University Arena.

As we pulled into the parking lot, we could see the massive crowd of people still waiting in line for the event. Some of them had been there for days—literally. Not even freezing temperatures and cold, wet snow could keep those warriors from seeing the leader of the free world. We've been attending Trump rallies for five years, and they never get old for us. They never get old for anyone who's attended one. But Trump people make enormous commitments to be at rallies, traveling from all over the country and following the president from event to event. It's sort of like the Deadheads who followed around the Grateful Dead in the 1970s, without the acid or tie-dyed shirts. One group of followers calls themselves "the Front Row Joes," and it's an apt description. They're always the first in line and have gone to dozens upon dozens of rallies. It's seeing people like the "Joes" that reminds us how lucky we are to be part of such an historic political phenomenon.

Together we'd been to hundreds of rallies, either backstage or in front-row seats reserved for us. A Trump rally really is the Greatest Show on Earth—there will never be anything else quite like it. And in front of us that night was another chance to see the president shine like no political star ever had.

He didn't disappoint. The fire marshal had to close the doors because the venue was over capacity, some 14,000 strong, a new record for the arena. Donald Trump, Jr., as usual, was one of the opening acts. Donny has become a massive draw in his own right. Trumpers love him—and Kimberly. That night the arena took to chanting "Forty-six, forty-six," letting him know that they were already thinking ahead to 2024.

Though we were concentrating on 2020, we couldn't help but think back to election-day eve, 2016. That night, SNHU was supposed to play host to 2016's final rally. But on the last day of a campaign, things rarely go according to plan. When Hillary decided to add a stop in North Carolina, the boss ordered us back onto the plane for one more stop—the last in a string of rallies that doubled the number of the events Hillary held. The election-day rally in Grand Rapids, Michigan, held in the wee hours of the morning on November 8, saw 14,000 faithful packed into an arena for one last glimpse of the man who promised to fight for middle America if the voters gave him the chance. Just hours later, Donald Trump would win the state of Michigan by 10,704 votes. Looking back on it, it might have been the most consequential rally of the entire campaign. It sure showed one thing: Donald Trump didn't take any vote or state for granted. He'd fight until the very last.

President Trump walked onstage in Manchester at approximately 7:03 p.m. and proceeded to give a raucous, stem-winding speech. As he always does, the president recognized the efforts of the people who support him. When he gave us a shout-out, we received a loud ovation. For Corey, with his family at his side, it was especially memorable.

Though the boss was at the top of his game, he ended the rally in just under an hour. Most of his rallies, especially ones like this where the audience is going wild, last much longer than that. We had a suspicion that something was up, but when we talked to some of the boss's senior advisors, no one seemed to know.

—————————

The next day, February 11, 2020, Dave was up early and drove to Corey's home in Windham. The plan was to head out to polling sites from there. Alison, Corey's wife, greeted Dave and the rest of the team, at the door.

"I'm starved," Dave said jokingly. "Where's breakfast?"

Alison shot Corey a look filled with daggers. He hadn't told her that the gang would be eating breakfast with them. Corey just shrugged his shoulders; it wasn't a surprise to her that Corey had planned something she didn't know about. We didn't have time for a full sit-down breakfast, anyway. It was election day, so we grabbed a couple of health bars and a couple of Monster energy drinks and headed out the door. Outside it was cold, in the thirties, but Corey wore his 2016 campaign "Team Trump" windbreaker. Like a baseball player on a hitting streak, he wasn't going to start experimenting with different bats. Dave took one look at him and shook his head.

The first stop was Windham High School, the town's polling location. Corey could have made the eight-minute drive with his eyes closed. His children go to the school for extra-curricular activities. He had also arranged for candidate Trump to speak there in 2016. We jumped out of the SUV, with Corey walking ahead. As he was just about to step into the high school to vote, Dave called after him.

"They're not going to let you in wearing that," Dave said.

Corey turned and flipped him the finger. "You'll see," he quipped. Of course, Dave was right. Electioneering rules in New Hampshire, and most other states, prohibit the use of campaign buttons, stickers, or, in Corey's case, a Trump windbreaker at polling sites. Corey walked out of the polling location with his windbreaker in hand.

The next polling site was Londonderry High School, about a ten-minute drive from Windham. On the way there, we made a pit stop at MaryAnn's Diner in Windham for a real breakfast. Corey knew just about everyone there, and we spent most of the time posing for selfies and listening to primary stories from when Herbert Hoover was president.

Back in the SUV, we did radio hits for both local and national stations—there is no such thing as downtime on election day. As we arrived at Londonderry High, we were struck by the size of the Trump tent in front; we half expected an elephant and a lion tamer to walk out of it. Al Baldasaro met us outside the tent. Along with being Trump 2020 campaign state cochairman and a legislator from Londonderry, Al is a legend in New Hampshire politics. We hit several more polling stops before heading to Radio Row in Manchester, also known as the "Queen City." One of the things that surprised us in making the polling rounds was the significant turnout of volunteers working on behalf of Mayor Pete on the Democrat side. Things wouldn't work out for the mayor of South Bend, but we have to admit that he put together a pretty good organization.

The turnout of volunteers for Bernie and Biden wasn't impressive at all. Though Bernie would end up squeaking out a victory over Mayor Pete, it wasn't by nearly the percentage he'd hoped to get. Before the primaries, pundits were telling everyone how Bernie's coalition was getting ready to take the Granite State by storm. The truth is, he was always just a niche candidate for socialists and far-left wackos. Though there are a lot of socialists and wackos in the Democrat Party, there were not enough in New Hampshire to provide him with the cushion needed to claim a decisive victory. The one piece of good news for Bernie was the miserable performance by Pocahontas. Senator Elizabeth Warren received just a little over 9 percent of the vote. That meager share came primarily from people who know her solely because New Hampshire borders her home state of Massachusetts. After the New Hampshire primary, the Warren campaign was on life support, and that's being generous. We were convinced that a one-on-one campaign between Bernie and the boss would be a blowout for us—we would crush him. However, after the way Sanders limped out of New Hampshire, the chances of that happening were dwindling quickly.

The biggest surprise, though, was Biden's performance. Though none of us expected him to win New Hampshire, we didn't think it would be as bad as it turned out for Sleepy Joe. We believed, as most political insiders did, that Joe was destined to be the Democrat nominee. We also thought he'd be President Trump's most formidable foe. Not many of us predicted that his campaign would crater the way it did in Iowa and New Hampshire. But in retrospect, we should have seen it coming. As the boss would say, Biden has lost a step. Probably more than one. Voters could see it in his performances in the Democrat primary debates. His responses were slow. Words would get jumbled in his mouth. His attitude was even worse; it was patently obvious that he was just going through the motions. Perhaps he thought he had the nomination all wrapped up. Maybe he knew the fix was in and they were never going to give it to Bernie Sanders. Or maybe, deep down, he knew his mind was fading and wouldn't be able to handle the most important job in the world.

In New Hampshire, however, the only thing he could think of doing was getting out of town. He didn't even stick around to pay his respects to his hardworking volunteers and staff from across the state. Instead, he hightailed it to South

Carolina at four in the afternoon, long before the polls even closed in New Hampshire. Believe us when we tell you that come November, the people of New Hampshire won't forget that Biden abandoned them. And it's our job to remind them of that every chance we get.

———————

The New Hampshire primary's Radio Row was located in the Radisson Hotel in Manchester. Each of us conducted multiple interviews there. In between interviews, Corey's cell phone rang. He could tell the call was coming from the White House. He tapped the green button, and it was the White House operator. She verified that it was Corey on the other end of the phone and then asked him to hold for a call from the vice president. The president calls Corey often, but Corey couldn't remember one single time over the course of the past three years that he had had a call from the vice president. Seconds later, the vice president's voice came over the line. He wanted to personally thank Corey for all he did for him and the president the day before while traveling in New Hampshire. Corey had arranged "The Cops for Trump" endorsement, helped secure the SNHU venue, and made sure the rally came off without a hitch. Though he was taken by the call and effusively expressed to Vice President Pence his gratitude for it, there was something on his mind—something he couldn't stop thinking about since the rally ended early the night before.

Without telling a single soul other than the people who needed to plan the trip, President Trump and Vice President Pence left Manchester and flew to Dover Air Force Base in Delaware. On a misty tarmac, with Air Force One and Air

Force Two parked in the distance, they saluted the flag-draped coffins of Sergeant First Class Javier Jaguar Gutierrez and Sergeant First Class Antonio Rey Rodriguez as they were being carried off a military plane. The soldiers had been killed a few days before in Afghanistan trying to mitigate a dispute when an Afghan soldier opened fire with a machine gun. You never know who your friends and allies truly are. The tragedy was especially painful to the president, who's been trying to end America's forever wars. In the weeks preceding the attack, the administration's peace envoy, Zalmay Khalilzad, had met several times with the Taliban in Qatar in the hope of hammering out a peace agreement. The president had angrily alluded to the murders during his State of the Union speech. Our soldiers, he had said, were not meant to be "law enforcement agencies" for other countries.

Both men were just twenty-eight.

The ceremony is called a "dignified transfer," and, along with visiting wounded soldiers at Walter Reed National Military Medical Center, it is for the president and vice president one of their most difficult and solemn duties. The president had cut the rally short so he could visit with the families as they waited for the C-17 military plane to arrive.

During the transfer of coffins from the transport to waiting vehicles, a mourner of one of the deceased broke free from those trying to hold her back and threw herself at the closing doors of the vehicle in an understandably emotional display. As we said, it's one of the president's and vice president's toughest jobs. The men and women in the armed forces who die for our freedom take precedence over politics every time. As is his way, the vice president took no credit. Instead, he just asked Corey to pray for the soldiers' families.

It came as no surprise, of course, that the president won the New Hampshire Republican primary. But the size of his victory was still shocking. Not since Ronald Reagan's 1984 reelection campaign had the New Hampshire primary been decided by such a large margin. And no other incumbent president, including Reagan, had received as many votes— more than twice the amount Biden got.

The results of the caucuses in Iowa were terrific. But New Hampshire showed we could bring the hammer down anytime we needed. At some point it dawned on us that we might be part of the most formidable campaign in the history of presidential politics.

South Carolina was next, and nothing, it seemed, could stop us. Little did we know what was about to hit our shores.

CHAPTER SIX

PURE AMERICAN GLORY

Soon, the cars will take to the track for the start. Tires will screech, rubber will burn, fans will scream and the great American race will begin.

—President Trump at the start of the Daytona 500

FEBRUARY 15, 2020

When Dave heard the president was going to be grand marshal at the 2020 Daytona 500, he thought it'd be great for a couple of reasons. NASCAR's most famous event of the year was what you'd call a "target-rich environment"—the organizers could have used a MAGA hat instead of a checkered flag and the crowd would have approved—big league. Be honest—it's a 150,000-person Trump rally with very large engines. But for Dave, the opportunities he saw for the president extended far beyond the cheap seats. Twelve million people or so would be watching at home on Fox. Every one of them would stop everything when the boss uttered the words "Start your engines." A towering American figure leading a legendary American event—those optics were something you cannot buy.

Presidential events like this can have a tendency to go sideways. More times than we could count, politicians, especially presidents and presidential hopefuls, have done more damage than good showing up at sporting events. In 1992, candidate Bill Clinton campaigned at the Darlington 500 and was resoundingly booed. The crowd at the 2009 Major League Baseball All-Star game jeered Obama big time in St. Louis. Even "Give 'Em Hell" Harry Truman got razzed at a Washington Senators game.

But more than any man holding the office before him, Donald Trump knows his audience. On November 9, 2019, the president attended the much-anticipated University of Alabama versus Louisiana State University football game in Tuscaloosa at the Bryant-Denny Stadium. If you know college football, you know how big the Crimson Tide–versus–Tigers game is. And if you know Donald Trump's fans, you can guess that there'd be more than a couple of them at the game.

Alabama is Trump Country and a special place in the history of the 2016 campaign. The first rally that really showed the world the force of the Trump movement took place in August 2015 at a football stadium in Mobile. More than 35,000 people packed the stadium for the chance to see the man promising to take on the establishment—and win. As Captain John Dunkin tipped the wings of Trump Force One, signaling the future president's arrival, our advance man, Mobile native George Gigicos, introduced the boss to the wildly screaming crowd. From that point on, Donald Trump could no longer be ignored. He shot all the way up to first in the polls and never looked back.

For Dave, the day was about as special as it could be. His daughter Isabella was a freshman at the University of Alabama, Tuscaloosa. You may not know this, but Dave has deep roots in Alabama. His wife, Susan, is from Marengo County. They have a family house there. And like many Alabama families, they are split between their love of Crimson Tide and Auburn Tigers football. They had long planned to attend this championship-level game. Though it was a hot ticket, Dave was able to acquire tickets for his family. When Dave found out the president was going to be there, he texted Mick Mulvaney and then White House political director Brian Jack and asked if he could stop by and see the president in the suite where he'd be watching the game. It was a big ask. It would have been one thing if it was just Dave or just Dave and Susan. However, out of respect for Dave and the work he had done for the president, the advance team called and told him it was all set for the family to meet with the president.

As far as the crowd's reaction at the LSU-Alabama game? Words on a page can't capture the feeling in the stadium that day. We encourage you, however, to google it. The noise level was off the charts. More than 100,000 screaming fans welcomed the president and first lady with a standing ovation that lasted almost five full minutes.

Daytona promised to be a day of opportunities for President Trump, and the campaign was hell-bent on squeezing his appearance at the famous track for everything it was worth. The White House put together some outstanding events for the boss that just seemed to get better as the day went on: a flyover by Air Force One with racing legend Darrell Waltrip on the plane; a TV spot of the president's speech before he announced "Start your engines!" to begin the race; the roar of the air force Thunderbirds streaking over Daytona; a victory lap around the track in the presidential limo, appropriately known as "the Beast."

You know, a real Trump-style appearance.

It hadn't all come together on its own. Dave had been responsible for getting Waltrip onto Air Force One. A couple of days before the race, he received a text from John Davis, an old friend of his from Bob Dole's 1988 presidential campaign. Davis asked Dave what he thought about putting the racing legend and the president together for the race. Dave's response was a short one: "Hell, yeah!"

What could be better? Waltrip is beloved among by racing fans. He'd just retired after nineteen years in the booth for NASCAR on Fox. He'd won the Daytona 500 in 1989 and was inducted into the NASCAR Hall of Fame in 2012. Having Waltrip with the president at the famous raceway would generate great press—and set Twitter on fire. It just so happened that the day before the race, February 14, Dave and Corey had lunch with President Trump in the White House. During the meal, Dave mentioned the idea to the Boss and, just as we'd thought, he loved it. Once the president approved, Dave reached out to Mick Mulvaney and set the plan into motion. Mulvaney even came up with the idea of having Darrell drive the Beast, but the Secret Service wouldn't let that happen. It would have been pretty cool, though.

That day, Dave was batting a thousand.

He'd been scrolling through Twitter the morning of the race when he'd come across a post by Hailie Deegan, a rising young female star on the NASCAR circuit. "Today's goal," she wrote. "Get my helmet signed by Trump."

"Oh, this is happening," Dave thought. That would be a great visual for the president.

Dave again texted Mick Mulvaney, but the chief of staff was in the air, flying to Stephen Miller's wedding. He also sent a text to Kimberly Guilfoyle and Don Jr., who he knew were traveling with the president to the race.

Don Jr. tweeted at Hailie shortly after:

DM me... I may know someone.

Just as the race was starting, someone forwarded us Don Jr.'s tweet. It was a photo of the president, the first lady, Kimberly, Don Jr., and Hailie Deegan. The text above the photo read, and we kid you not, "Promises Made... Promises Kept."

Absolute gold.

Unfortunately for the fans, heavy rain began to fall—and kept falling. After multiple starts and stops and a few laps completed, the race was postponed to the next day. At the end of a particularly exciting final lap, Denny Hamlin nosed out Ryan Blaney in the second closest finish in Daytona history. But you didn't need a photo finish to see the victory the president got that day.

By the end of February, it was hard to imagine a better trajectory for the 2020 campaign than the one we were on. The stars had aligned for the president: The economy was the best it had ever been in the history of our country. The soaring Dow Jones Industrial Average and the ballooning 401(k)s it fostered were the president's ticket to reelection. More satisfyingly, the Democrat Party had already proved its ineptness. While the billion-dollar Trump campaign was firing on all cylinders, the Democrats were yet to leave the starting line.

On February 26, Dave wrote and published an op-ed for Fox News detailing just how bad the candidates looked at the Democrat debate the night before. Think about this Democrats were so desperate many of them were considering Mike Bloomberg as their white knight. Mike Bloomberg! You know, the Republican mayor of New York. The guy who spent nearly a billion dollars to win one delegate from Guam. For a supposed "good" businessman, it would be the worst return on investment in American political history. The rest of the candidates didn't fare much better. Biden often looked confused and old. Minnesota senator Amy Klobuchar and Mayor Pete showed themselves as inexperienced. Elizabeth Warren was bitter and just plain nasty. Tom Steyer (if you remember him) was just another Bloomberg type, flushing his money down the drain, all for an ego trip. Watching them pile on poor Bernie almost made us feel sorry for him. Almost. The beginning of the end of Bernie Sanders was when his comrade Elizabeth Warren attacked him on the debate stage. We could see from that moment on that the fix was in and Sleepy Joe had been anointed as the nominee by the Democrat establishment, voters be damned. The bottom line was once it got down to Biden vs. Sanders, Democrat primary voters rejected the far-far-left socialist policies of Sanders in order to try to beat Donald Trump with someone they perceived as a more moderate candidate. The bad news for the Democrats is just like he did with Hillary, the president is going to mop the floor with their nominee. The only one who had any fund-raising momentum was crazy Bernie, and, let's face it, Bernie wasn't going to beat Donald Trump. Not in a million years.

Everything was falling into place. For the first time in four years since back during the 2016 campaign, Donald Trump wasn't being subjected to a phony investigation staged by the Democrats. You could almost see the spring in his step. He was always a counterpuncher, but now the presidnet no longer had to fight with one hand tied behind his back.

On Sunday morning, March 1, both our phones buzzed at the same time. Brian Jack, the White House political director, had sent this text:

"All set. Be on West Exec at 2:45pm for a 3pm departure."

"West Exec" is West Executive Avenue, the short block that runs between the Eisenhower Executive Office Building and the White House. The departure meant on Air Force One. We were back in full swing of campaign season and heading to North Carolina for the biggest reelection rally yet.

As it normally goes, we both had meetings that morning in Washington. Corey had breakfast at the Hay-Adams hotel with RNC chair Ronna Romney McDaniel and Richard Walters, the RNC's chief of staff. Dave spent the morning in meetings at his office at Citizens United. We regrouped, as always, with just enough time to make it to the White House.

Our entrance into the world's most famous building isn't a complete delight to everyone who works there, but it's a thrill for us. It's sort of like the scene from the movie *Goodfellas*. You know, the one where Henry Hill walks through the Copacabana's kitchen to a table reserved for him right in front of the stage? And some inside the building—like John Kelly, for instance—are jealous of our relationship with the president.

Though we've been in the West Wing dozens of times, we never take it for granted. These are the halls where Abraham Lincoln and Ronald Reagan walked—where global decisions were made and wars have been won. But amid all the reverence for the past, there are times however, when our visits to the White House are a bit unusual.

A few days before that visit, Corey received a package from Goose Gossage, the great Yankee relief pitcher with the blond handlebar mustache. For those of you who don't remember, Goose played for the Yankees during the late 1970s and early 1980s, a time when the Yankees were known as the "Bronx Zoo" for their antics off the field. Back then, the Boss was a frequent visitor to Yankee Stadium, often sitting in Yankee owner George Steinbrenner's box. He knew most of the players by name, including Goose. The package from Gossage contained a personally autographed bat from his induction ceremony into the Baseball Hall of Fame, along with a note thanking the president for his unwavering leadership. He also wanted Corey to let him know the next time the boss would be holding a rally in Colorado, where he lives, so he could experience the phenomenon himself.

Now, we weren't sure how many people before us walked into the White House with a baseball bat, but we imagine it had to be a pretty short list.

When the Secret Service agent saw Corey place the box with the bat on the conveyor belt to be X-rayed, he turned to his partner.

"Can they come in here with that?" he asked.

"Yeah," his partner replied. "These guys can."

Please don't get the wrong idea. We know that it's an honor to count the president of the United States as a friend. We don't take it for granted. But we also knew that as a true sports fan, he would treasure what we were bringing him.

Like most friendships, our relationship with the boss is contingent on trust and mutual respect. "Good friends are like stars—you don't always see them, but you know they're always there." No words sum up our relationship with the president better. Still, we are also keenly aware that our relationship with the boss isn't the same as it was during the 2016 campaign. When your friend becomes president of the United States, the nature of the relationship has to change.

With Corey carrying Goose's bat, we made the rounds of the White House complex. We stopped by to say hi to Mick Mulvaney. The White House chief of staff's office is one of the largest, second in size only to the president's. It also has a fireplace that Mulvaney liked to keep roaring all the time. It's a nice touch on a cold day, since   believe it or not—the White House can get pretty drafty. We spent a few moments with Peter Navarro, the president's trade director, and Larry Kudlow, the boss's top economic advisor. Larry had been fighting some health issues but now looked at the top of his game, and we were all very happy about that. A little over an hour later, we were again boarding Air Force One for the short flight to

Charlotte, North Carolina, where the president was to hold a rally. It would be his last—at least for a while. And none of us had any way of knowing.

Once on the plane, we sat with Pam Bondi, a former Florida attorney general. Fresh off a fabulous job as part of the president's impeachment defense team, Pam had just finished up her role in the White House. Ronna McDaniel, the RNC chairwoman, was also with us, as was our old friend Stephen Miller, who'd just been married two weeks before. Earlier in the day, Corey had had a conversation with Ronna. She asked him if he thought Dave would be interested in being the vice chairperson of the Republican National Convention. It would obviously be a high honor, and Corey told Ronna he thought Dave would be thrilled.

Most of the rest of the talk aboard Air Force One was about Joe Biden and his comeback in the South Carolina primary. It wasn't like the turnaround in his campaign caught us off guard. We had been ready for Beijing Biden since day one, when he was the front-runner and just about everyone's pick to be the Democrat nominee. We also knew that as a candidate, Sleepy Joe had some significant flaws. One of the bigger ones is his inappropriate touching of women. The long list of his odd activities includes long hugs, shoulder rubs, and the credible assault accusations of Tara Reade. Then there's the tale of his staring down the swimming pool gangsta Corn Pop. If you want a laugh, google that one. The point is, there are plenty of skeletons in Biden's closet for us to bring out. With more than fifty years in the Swamp, Joe Biden's dealings and his son Hunter's business activities are easy targets.

We were ready for Biden.

What we, and the rest of the planet, hadn't counted on, was the deadly virus we all had to face.

On Friday, March 6, Dave took an evening flight from DC to Tampa. Griffin goes to school in Sarasota and was playing in a golf tournament that weekend. It's always a balance between work and family for us. For Dave, who now has college-age children, it means many extra sky miles on his credit card. After watching Griffin's match Saturday morning, he made the three-hour drive across to Mar-a-Lago.

Now, being president of Citizens United and an outside advisor to the president is not the easiest job in the world. But it's not like we're carrying bricks for a living. Case in point: that Saturday night we had the pleasure of attending Kimberly Guilfoyle's fiftieth birthday celebration at the president's beachside resort. Tough work if you can get it, right?

Corey and Dave met at the Courtyard Marriott in West Palm Beach and took one car over to the club.

Joining us for Kimberly's party were a number of political heavyweights, including former New York mayor Rudy Giuliani, Fox News host Tucker Carlson, Senator Lindsey Graham, Turning Point USA founder Charlie Kirk, congressman Matt Gaetz, Acting Director of National Intelligence Richard Grenell, and Trump 2020 senior advisor Katrina Pierson.

After dinner, Kimberly's party expanded to the pool area, where we met up with our friend Andrew Giuliani, public liaison assistant to the president and son of America's mayor. He'd texted us earlier in the day to say he'd be bringing along a couple of special guests. One of them was Ryan Zimmerman, the first baseman for the world champion Washington Nationals. The other was retired Nationals great, Jayson Werth. Dave and Jayson actually had something in common: their sons attend the same school in Sarasota. Though the conversation with the baseball stars was light and breezy, Dave, the consummate political pro, never lets an opportunity pass him by. Noting his charm and name recognition, he asked Zimmerman if he would consider a run for Virginia governor. Zimmerman laughed, as did the rest of us, but he would be a great candidate. After all, he wouldn't be the first guy we know with zero political experience to shake up the status quo.

Though Kimberly rightfully drew much of the attention that night, most of the attendees were waiting for the president to make his appearance. While we were by the pool, the boss and Melania were having dinner on the club's terrace with President Jair Bolsonaro of Brazil. At the table with them were Bolsonaro's son Eduardo, Ivanka, Jared, National Security Advisor Robert O'Brien and his wife, Lo-Mari, the Brazilian president's press secretary, Fabio Wajngarten, and Nestor Forster, Bolsonaro's top diplomat in Washington.

Before that evening, we wouldn't have been able to tell you those last two names if you had given us four vowels and five spins. But soon after, just about everyone in the country knew who they were.

When the boss, flanked by President Bolsonaro, walked into the ballroom, he was met with thunderous applause and shouts of "Four more years." He gave Kimberly a heartfelt toast and then began to mingle with the guests. Robert O'Brien came over to say hello and thank us. We had both

made calls to support his being appointed as the national
security advisor, which we were happy to do. He's definitely
on the team.

Both of us had had a long day, so we ended up leaving
before the party's end. News about coronavirus had been
popping up more frequently, so it was on our minds as we
headed out of Mar-a-Lago. Just a few days later, the Bolsonaro administration announced that the Brazilian president's
press secretary and diplomat had both tested positive for
Covid-19. To the best of our recollection, we hadn't come too
close to either of them—but we certainly had conversations
with people who had. The idea of it was disconcerting, to say
the least.

Dave had taken the news about the coronavirus particularly
seriously. As a nearly twenty-year veteran of the fire service in
Montgomery County, Maryland, and trained as an EMT-B,
he'd had an inner alarm bell going off in his head ever since
he heard the first news coming out of China. He expected the
coronavirus to get much, much worse. On March 3, he met
Mark Meadows for lunch at the Capitol Hill Club, a common meeting place for congressmen and other Washington
insiders. Usually, Dave and Mark would eat from the buffet,
which is rather good. This time, however, Dave told Mark
they should avoid the buffet and order from the menu, just
to be safe. He gave the congressman a short dissertation on
how easily a virus can spread—especially in open food service and communal settings. By the time Dave was finished,
the congressman had flagged a waiter and they both ordered
hamburgers.

Dave had a good reason to be cautious. About eight years earlier, he had had a minor heart attack at forty-six and later developed an infection in his heart called endocarditis. The infectious disease team at MedStar Washington Hospital Center worked around the clock to diagnose and treat him. The treatment had required almost three months of IV antibiotics, twenty-four hours a day. After all that, they performed open-heart surgery on him to repair his mitral valve. Since then, he's been diagnosed with a painful autoimmune disease that requires him to take medication to suppress his immune system. And to top it all off, he had just recently started taking a medication for high blood pressure. The combination of those factors placed him in the category at high risk of dying from the coronavirus if he should contract it.

A week later, he would have another close call.

On March 10, Ronna McDaniel met Dave at the same restaurant. She wanted to officially offer him the position of vice chair of the Republican National Convention. They caught up on several important topics before she offered Dave the position, which he gratefully accepted.

A few days later, Ronna was in self-imposed quarantine, showing potential symptoms of the virus. She'd also been a guest at Kimberly's party and had come into contact with the Brazilian delegation. When Dave called to check on her, she was feeling horrible and had yet to hear back on her test for Covid-19. After what felt like an eternity, the result finally came in: Ronna tested negative. For Ronna and Dave, this moment came as a big relief. But beyond that, the episode served as a warning sign that we needed to take this virus seriously.

Over the next few days, the entire world was turned upside down. Scientists were tracking the virus to China's meat, fish, and other "wet" goods markets located right across from the Wuhan Institute of Virology, China's first level 4 biosafety lab. But by then the virus had not only spread throughout Europe but also had come to our shores.

Covid-19, as the disease had come to be called, stopped Washington dead in its tracks. One day, we were running to the airport like every other day, living out of a suitcase, using up battery life in our phones like there were holes in them, and then . . . nothing. At least it seemed that way.

On March 11, the president announced he was canceling rallies in Nevada, Colorado, and Wisconsin. The next day, he barred noncitizen travel from Europe. He had already stopped travel from China in January when the outbreak first occurred, but greater measures clearly needed to be taken. Annual traditions such as the Gridiron Club Dinner, the Washington Press Club Foundation dinner, and the White House Correspondents' Dinner were canceled. The US Capitol Complex was shut to the public. Several Republican senators were in quarantine after attending the Conservative Political Action Conference (CPAC) and coming into contact with someone who tested positive for the virus. In the coming weeks, the entirety of Washington, DC's, political machinery essentially ground to a halt. For us, our trip to Charlotte on March 11 to meet with the Republican National Convention team would be our last political event for a long time. We took extreme precautions for the trip, wiping down the seats on the plane before getting on and bringing copious amounts of hand sanitizer with us. This would be the last trip for us until the virus was under control. Corey called his wife during the trip and told her they should consider taking the kids out of school until further notice—just in case.

At the end of the trip, we headed home. As was the case for millions of other Americans, our priority was our families.

For those of us who know him, it came as no surprise that Dave had already planned for something like this. After back-to-back hurricanes hit Maryland many years ago, he bought two huge plastic storage crates and filled them with emergency supplies. He hadn't checked them for a couple of years, though. When he did in early March, he was surprised at what he had, including medical-grade masks and toilet paper, which were in scarce supply! The crates also contained a first aid kit, a battery-operated radio, and a bottle of Tylenol that expired in 2013. He threw out everything that had passed its expiration date, jumped into his truck, and headed out for supplies. At Safeway, he filled a shopping cart with essentials. With enough food to feed a family for a couple of weeks, he headed to Bass Pro Shop for ammo. Back home, Isabella and Griffin, Dave's two oldest children, stacked it all in the lockers, safely tucked away.

Corey, too, has first-responder experience. He graduated from the New Hampshire police academy in 2006 and served four years in law enforcement. Now his cop instincts reemerged. In the Lewandowski household, it was Alison who went for provisions. She made several trips to buy bulk supplies for a long confinement period. Corey spent the time preparing his property. His house, at the end of a dead-end road, sits on four acres that front a small pond. He checked the security cameras positioned around the property and made sure that the well, which supplies the water for the house, was in working order. He then checked to see if he had enough firewood, ammunition, and cash. Like Dave, Corey is a gun enthusiast, maybe even more so. He brought two of his boys,

Alex and Reagan, down to the safe to give them a refresher course on gun use and safety. They cleaned and assembled the guns, making sure they were in perfect working condition before closing the door behind them, ready for whatever was to come.

The number one job for every American father is to protect his family, and we were no different.

Still, as the days went by, we couldn't help but think about how the virus had impacted the president's reelection campaign.

We believed the Trump campaign was an unstoppable force. We had the money, the expertise, state-of-the-art digital capacity, formidable senior campaign staff, and a sprawling network of volunteers and other supporters. The digital campaign would survive—thrive, actually—in the days ahead. But the boots-on-the-ground campaign and the rallies were ghosts of politics past—at least for the foreseeable future.

This new political world was going to take a little getting used to.

Throughout the first part of this book, we have given you a lot of flashbacks to 2016, which was maybe the greatest campaign ever run. We could have traveled halfway to the moon with the miles we logged on Trump Force One. The thought of not being on the road in 2020 was nearly unfathomable.

Still, we had one indispensable component that remained from the 2016 campaign, an element that had only gotten better with time.

That component, of course, was President Donald J. Trump, the Promises he's made, and the Promises he's kept.

★

The United States has been losing, for many years, 600 to 800 Billion Dollars a year on Trade. With China we lose 500 Billion Dollars. Sorry, we're not going to be doing that anymore!

       —@realDonaldTrump, May 6, 2019

★

CHAPTER SEVEN

IT'S THE ECONOMY—
AND CHINA—STUPID

On April 28, 2011, Donald Trump flew into Las Vegas to give a speech at the Treasure Island Hotel & Casino, a big resort on the Vegas strip owned by his friend of many years Phil Ruffin. A little over five years later, Ruffin would take the stage at the 2016 Republican National Convention in Cleveland, Ohio, to give a ringing endorsement of Mr. Trump, telling the delegates on the floor that "his handshake is better than any contract you will ever write." Back on that April day, the two men were real estate developers with successful hotels on the Vegas strip. Rumors of a possible presidential run were in the air, but nobody had a sense of how serious they were.

So when the future president of the United States took the stage, nobody in the audience knew quite what to expect. They knew it'd be a performance, but content-wise, it was anybody's guess. What they saw blew them all away: Donald Trump stepped up to the podium, joked around with the audience for a while, and then bent over the microphone like a master sculptor over a solid block of marble. As we've written before, it was always during speeches like those— the Lincoln Day dinners, the Freedom Summits, the off-the-cuff addresses to small political groups—that Donald Trump honed his rhetorical chops. While he was speaking, he could test his policies in real time and come up with incredible slogans on the fly. His address that night, given to the Clark County Republicans, was no different.

In fact, if you haven't seen the speech, we highly recommend you take a look. It's still archived on C-SPAN, right under a bold warning about "offensive language." What you'll find is not just a crystal-clear articulation of what President Trump believes to this day; it's a master class in captivating an audience from arguably the greatest and most entertaining public speaker of his time. Throughout the ninety-minute performance, delivered with the comedic timing of someone well versed in stand-up, the future president laid out his entire first-term agenda: trade policy and the military, the repeal of NAFTA—quintessential points that became the message of "America First." But he also touched on other things: the upcoming race for the White House—topics to generate controversy and interest. Anyone who's ever said President Trump doesn't care about policy clearly never heard him give a speech in those early days.

Around the twenty-eight-minute mark of the speech, with the crowd practically eating out of his hand, Mr. Trump turned his attention to an issue that would come to define his first term: Communist China. After telling the crowd about how much money he had made doing deals with the Chinese, how he'd found ways around their crooked rules and bent their state-run Communist banks to his will, Trump went on the offensive.

"It always gets back to China," said the future president. "While we are busy being the policemen of the world, China is spending a billion dollars a day *buying* the world. . . . I'd tell you what I'd do: drop a twenty-five percent tax on China . . . but the messenger is important. I could have one man say, 'We're going to tax you twenty-five percent.'" (You can't tell from seeing it printed, but this is where Trump put on a whiny, high-pitched voice and waved his hands in the air, causing the crowd to break into uproarious laughter. Imagine it's one of the true-blue Washington "experts"—such as Beijing Biden.)

From there, the president slipped into the voice we would all come to know and love during the 2016 campaign: the brash, tough-talking New York developer from Queens. "Or I could say, 'Listen, you motherfuckers, we're going to tax you twenty-five percent.' You've said the same thing, but it's a different message!"

The crowd knew how right he was.

It just goes to show that even back in 2011, President Trump knew that Communist China posed a serious threat— to both the United States and the world. As he would say time and again during the 2016 campaign, China's economic aggression was destroying our economy and manufacturing base, with more than 5 million manufacturing jobs gone and over 50,000 factories lost. Lopsided trade deals culminated in a massive $500 billion trade deficit that sucked the lifeblood out of America—all with the approval of our Washington "experts." The various forms of China's economic aggression would come to be known during the Trump administration as China's "Seven Deadly Sins," providing the foundation for the tariffs and other trade protective measures put into place to level the economic playing field.

These Seven Deadly Sins—practiced to this day—don't carry the label lightly: brazen intellectual property theft to the tune of hundreds of billions of dollars a year, forced technology transfer policies fleecing American businesses operating in China, blatant cyberhacking of American trade secrets and data, pernicious currency manipulation that jacks up Chinese exports to the United States while suppressing US exports to China, and the exportation of deadly fentanyl to our country that has killed nearly a million Americans. For decades, the United States has suffered from a systematic weakening at the hands of the Chinese—and President Trump was the first one to do anything about it.

In his historic June 2016 jobs plan speech, arguably one of the best speeches of the campaign, candidate Trump made it clear he would put a quick end to China's economic aggression: "If China does not stop its illegal activities, including its theft of American trade secrets, I will use every lawful presidential power to remedy trade disputes, including the application of tariffs consistent with Section 201 and 301 of the Trade Act of 1974 and Section 232 of the Trade Expansion Act of 1962." Another promise made and another promise kept. If leaders in government for the past forty years (we're looking at you, Joe) had had even half the insight of candidate Trump, we would never have been in this situation.

Back on the day he gave that speech in Las Vegas in 2011, the Chinese government was indeed spying on its citizens, manipulating its currency, and violating human rights inside its borders. Anyone with half a brain could have seen that it was only a matter of time before something terrible happened to the United States. But back then, no one in the elite political class cared. Not Barack Obama. Not Joe Biden. Not the legislators on Capitol Hill on either side of the aisle. No one.

These were the old-fashioned globalist days when the powerful elites clung to the notion that if you engaged with China economically, the brutal, repressive, authoritarian nightmare would morph into some kind of democratic, peaceful dream. Icons such as Henry Kissinger, who made tens of millions of dollars off the CCP, were writing books such as his *On China*, which claimed we should seek to understand the Chinese instead of resisting their advances, which were fundamentally at odds with the West.

But even then, there were others writing books with quite the opposite view, authors like Peter Navarro with his *The Coming China Wars: Where They Will Be Fought and How They Can Be Won* in 2006 and *Death by China: Confronting the Dragon—a Global Call to Action* in 2011; also Michael Pillsbury's *The Hundred-Year Marathon: China's Secret Strategy to Replace America as the Global Superpower*. Those piercing China critiques, widely scorned by the globalist elites at the time, were read by Donald J. Trump—and today, these books read more like the government reports now warning of the China threat.

Most people probably don't remember when Mitt Romney, of all people, released his fifty-nine-point economic plan as a candidate in 2012. Believe it or not, it included a plan to get pretty tough on the Chinese—not nearly as tough as President Trump would get four years later, of course, but much more than anyone else was proposing.

As soon as that plan was released, the *New York Times* wrote, "Among all the elements of Mitt Romney's 59-point economic plan, his vow to crack down on China's trade policy would seem the most out of place." That was the same elitist horseshit they would later throw at candidate Trump in 2016. It was just as ridiculous then as it would be four years later. The elite pundit class said that Romney didn't understand the inner workings of the world economy, that he couldn't possibly make the Chinese Communist Party pay up, and that attacking the CCP like that could, as the *New York Times* put it, "set off a counterproductive trade war that would damage the United States economy."

Sound familiar?

Even the *Wall Street Journal*, which is usually the most pro-Republican of the Fake News outlets, published an op-ed titled "Romney's China Blunder," which quoted well-known economists from all over the political spectrum to warn why a trade war could never work. "Once a U.S. President starts whipping up trade furies," wrote the editorial board, "it's hard to predict how the story ends. Congress already has a bipartisan lineup pressing to impose 25-percent tariffs on all Chinese goods. Because every administration also needs Beijing's support on a range of global issues, candidate Romney would be wiser to promise to pressure China to speed up its financial reform and pledging American help to make the process easier."

In other words, a kumbaya of incompetence. *Can't we all just get along?*

The *Wall Street Journal* was wrong then, and they'd be wrong four years later when it published basically the same op-ed in 2016. But unlike Trump, Mitt Romney didn't have the *cajones* to call the paper out on it. He capitulated instead. He walked back his position like a true, useless establishment politician. During the final presidential debate of the 2012 election cycle, when he was pushed on the issue of China, he delivered his final kowtow to the authoritarians: "We can be a partner with China. We don't have to be an adversary in any way, shape, or form." He never brought it up again. Soon after, Barack Obama would mop the floor with the weakling on election night. Romney had some of the right ideas, but he didn't have the conviction to stick with them when it mattered most. But as the saying goes, the road to Hell is paved with good intentions.

Today, most people might be surprised to learn that Donald Trump endorsed Romney in February 2012 at the Trump Hotel, only a few miles down the Vegas strip from where he spoke that night in 2011. Uncharacteristically for him, Donald Trump did not get a great return on his investment that night. Romney abandoned his original position because he'd thought he had to win over the journalists and elite economists instead of fighting for working-class Americans whose lives and businesses had been decimated by China. Because of that, Mr. 47-Percent lost big time, leaving us with the panda bear politics of Barack Obama and Beijing Joe Biden for four more years. The Obama/Biden merry band of acolytes made sure that nobody even thought about getting tough on China. Instead, they opened negotiations with Asian countries, trying to send a vague signal that the United States wanted to exert influence in Asia, too, if China would allow it—complete capitulation.

The one time Obama feigned tough action on China, CCP general secretary Xi Jinping came to the Rose Garden and signed a deal promising that China would stop its cyberhacking of US businesses and cease its militarization of the South China Sea. As with all things China, the deal wasn't worth the paper it was signed on. Obama and Biden got snookered, and their allies in the media didn't care one lick.

BREAKING THE CHAIN

From the first weeks of the campaign, President Trump saw the importance of China beyond being a key to solving our economic woes. This issue could unlock the blue states of the "Rust Belt," long loyal to Democrats. Looking at the United States like a business, Trump could tell that we had far too much exposure to the Chinese. We were too reliant on them for steel, prescription drugs, and far too many other things— and China's economic aggression made it impossible for the United States to compete fairly.

Instead of doing economic studies or hiring a bunch of Washington consultants to write position papers, Donald Trump started spreading his message about China to the people who wanted to hear it the most. He did this by participating in hundreds of hour-long interviews with radio and television hosts, most notably Steve Bannon, who at the time had a very popular drive-time radio show on SiriusXM called *Breitbart News Daily*. As we've written before, it was during these interviews with Bannon, Hugh Hewitt, Sean Hannity, and others that Trump learned how to take a message that had been outside the mainstream of the Republican Party for decades and distill it into a few simple, digestible phrases.

In that cauldron of learning, Trump listened while the hosts talked, analyzing their every utterance in real time.

This enabled him to figure out how to bring that message to the American people. This is part of the reason why, when we were preparing for a big debate, we'd always be sure to have Donald Trump go a few rounds with Bill O'Reilly on television or radio. Despite his personal issues, O'Reilly was one hell of an interviewer; he never let Trump get off easy on a question. Coming out of an interview with him, Donald Trump would always be firing on all cylinders. When he talked China with Bill O'Reilly, we always knew he was working out the kinks in his argument, preparing it for the main stage of the general election.

Then, as the campaign wore on, Trump brought his warnings about the reliance of our economy on China from the fringes to the mainstream. When the message was refined and word choice perfect, he was in an ideal position to start educating the American public. One of the most memorable interviews came on August 24, 2015, when Trump did one of his famous "phoners" on *Fox & Friends*.

During that show, Steve Doocy read Trump, then the front-runner for the Republican nomination, a quote from a newspaper columnist who'd published a piece about him the day before. It read, "Investors and financial journalists scrambling to find an explanation for the recent plunge in global stock markets have plenty of suspects. . . . Personally, I blame the decline in share values on Donald Trump. Trump's policies are the opposite of the pro-growth approach." The author of those words, Ira Stoll, was as wrong then as he is now.

Thanks to his long hours on the radio, the president had a perfect line ready to go. "Wow," he said. "That's amazing. He blames me. I'm the one telling everybody what's going wrong and what's going to go wrong. And frankly, I'm the one that says you better start uncoupling from China because China has problems and they have *big* problems and they're going to bring us down. So, for this guy, I never heard of him. I have no idea who he is. He's probably not very good at what he does. But to blame me is incredible because I'm the one that says uncouple."

Sure, that might sound pretty simple. But that is the secret to presidential politics.

During the entire 2016 campaign, our candidate beat the drum about China so loudly that his unique, percussive way of pronouncing the country's name turned into a joke. (Reading that sentence just now, you probably tried to do it in your head. Go ahead, it's fun! *Chiy*-na. *CHIY*-na!) It might be funny to you, but like everything the president does, it's calculated. He makes people remember what he's saying. The same goes for his tough-guy language out on the stump. We remember all his best lines and most outrageous speeches to this day, and in turn, we remember the message he was trying to get out.

On July 21, 2015, talking about the Obama administration's negotiations with China, he asked, "Why are you doing state dinners with them? . . . Just take them to McDonald's and go back to the negotiating table." On November 3, he said, "These are fiercre people in terms of negotiation. They want to take your throat out, they want to cut you apart. These are tough people. . . . they have taken advantage of us like nobody in history. It's the greatest theft in the history of the world what they've done to the United States." On April 17, 2016: "China is upset because of the way Donald Trump is talking about trade with China. They're ripping us off folks! It's time. I'm so happy they're upset. They haven't been upset with us in thirty years!"

We could go on, but you probably get the point. The fact of the matter is this: in light of recent events, we think it's important to point out just how long President Trump has been trying to warn us about the dangers of failing to deal with China and its totalitarian Communist government. The whole time he was running for president, he knew that our reliance on China for products like medicine, raw materials for manufacturing, and medical supplies put us at an extreme risk. He knew years in advance that if anything ever happened to the Chinese economy—say, a brand-new global pandemic that no one had ever seen before—we would be, in a word, screwed. Big league. As our political idol Lee Atwater might put it, this guy could see around corners. He tried to warn us all what was coming. If only we'd listened then, when we still had time.

GOING MAINSTREAM

When Donald Trump first started talking about China on the campaign stage, the pundits class went nuts all over again. It was the same as it had been with Mitt Romney, except this time, the message came in an even more brash, offensive package. For them, it was Armageddon. They had made fun of the last Republican who talked about getting tough on China—a mild-mannered guy who would never have been tough enough no matter what—and in return, they got Donald Trump, who couldn't possibly have cared less what the pundits had to say. No matter how much the "experts" complained, they couldn't get Donald Trump to walk back a single one of his positions.

None of the pundits could understand why, with all the life-and-death problems we were facing in 2016—global warming and (*gasp!*) the use of *plastic drinking straws*—we should take time out to worry about the Communist government of China. There were calls that we needed to come together as a nation, not get farther apart. It seemed as though there was nobody in the world who was willing to listen to what Trump was saying besides the voters.

Then, one afternoon in 2016, Corey was in the back of a taxi around Lexington and 3rd Avenue in Manhattan. He'd just left his apartment and was heading back to the office in Trump Tower for a few more hours. The cab driver had the radio tuned to NPR, and the host was conducting an interview about China and trade policy. In those days, Corey didn't have much time to use the bathroom, let alone listen to the radio or read for pleasure.

After a minute or two, Corey realized that the man being interviewed was a professor from the University of California, Irvine, named Peter Navarro, who has a PhD from Harvard and some of the same ideas about trade with China that Mr. Trump had. When the cab reached its destination, Corey actually asked the cabbie to let the meter run and turn up the radio so he could keep listening to Dr. Navarro.

He was shocked that NPR had even allowed Peter on in the first place. But as it turned out, Navarro had some impressive credentials—real credentials. Aside from the Harvard

PhD, he'd published several books on China and had directed a searing movie, *Death by China*, based on his book of the same title. Narrated by Martin Sheen, the movie stands as the definitive critique of the devastation China wrought after Bill Clinton and a Republican Congress let China join the World Trade Organization.

Corey didn't know any of that at the time. He was just riveted by Navarro's radio interview and thought it would be great to have him on board the Trump campaign. By the time he heard the interview, Navarro had already been in touch directly with Mr. Trump via his personal assistant, Rhona Graff. He and Mr. Trump had talked about China on numerous occasions. So when Jared Kushner suggested publishing a policy paper on China, he and Corey knew there was only one person for the job.

They decided to bring Navarro into the fold. Throughout the campaign, we'd ask him questions and task him with helping craft the message on how to decouple our economy from China's. It's not like he was working in the New York office or helping decide policy, of course. Even if he wanted to do that, it would have been pointless. In the early days, all the ideas came straight from the mind of Donald J. Trump. Just like today, the president would talk to people he respects, absorb the information they gave him, and then make the calls completely on his own. But having a well-respected scholar like Navarro on the team appeased the liberal media—for a few seconds, at least.

As soon as we announced that Navarro had something to do with the Trump campaign, the geniuses in the media pounced on him. All at once, none of his scholarship or published position papers were worth anything to them. He was on Team Trump, and therefore he was wrong. John Oliver, a liberal talk show host, did an entire segment on how wrong Navarro was about China.

The thing about Peter, though, is that his credentials are unimpeachable. The guy has forgotten more about world affairs than most of those jokers will ever know. The country is lucky to have him in the White House today, and the attacks on him only serve to illustrate the extent of the media's Trump Derangement Syndrome. One day, he's a widely respected scholar; the next day, he's a pariah—all because he supported candidate Donald Trump. But some things, as Peter knows, are just too important to care what the media thinks.

DECOUPLING

The best way to make the haters shut up—for a little while, at least—is by winning. So that's exactly what we did.

Once President Trump won the White House, it was Navarro and a small team of experts he assembled who led the charge against our reliance on China for goods and services. While always at war internally with globalists such as Gary Cohn, the team helped the president implement his agenda and begin cutting ties with the Chinese economy for good. Along with US Trade Representative Robert Lighthizer, Commerce Secretary and longtime Trump friend Wilbur Ross, and Steve Bannon, these China experts fundamentally transformed the way Republicans think about China. Before Trump, the GOP was like everyone else; it was full of people who made money hand over fist dealing with the Communist Party of China and their state-run banks. None of them had any incentive to rock the boat. President Trump changed all that.

But it wasn't easy. Trump was met with enormous resistance, particularly within his own White House. From the Never Trump wing of the building, Wall Street executives such as the aforementioned "Globalist" Gary Cohn, who made money at Goldman Sachs under the old be-nice-to-China system for years, was at the top of the list.

You might remember Gary as the source of Bob Woodward's book *Fear: Trump in the White House*, in which Cohn stated that he and Rob Porter, the disgraced former staff secretary, removed papers from the Resolute Desk to stop the president from destroying the world's economy. Luckily, Cohn was as wrong about that as he was about China. The same goes for other establishment Republicans who tried to get the president to weaken his aggressive stance on China.

Aside from China, there were other significant trade accomplishments. President Trump drastically revised our trade relationship with South Korea to benefit the United States, completely retooling Hillary Clinton's disgraceful United States–Korea Free Trade Agreement. (The president, along with his team led by Jared Kushner, renegotiated NAFTA—the worst trade deal in US history—and replaced it with the far more pro-America USMCA). For his work in finalizing the replacement agreement, Kushner was awarded the Order of the Aztec Eagle, the country's highest honor bestowed upon a foreigner, by the Mexican president for a job well done.

When the president first floated the idea of imposing tariffs on China, there was an outcry among the elite political class. You'll remember the screeching arguments: imposing tariffs would destabilize the economy; a trade war would be notoriously hard to win. I'm sure they were averting their eyes when President Trump, making good on his promise from seven years earlier, slapped a 25 percent tax on Chinese imports. Contrary to media belief, the tariffs weren't just random acts of aggression; they were worked out in detail by Lighthizer and Navarro, the first real experts to work in Washington in a long time, and were perfectly calibrated to apply pressure to China.

Of course China retaliated. No one expected any less. But Trump, as the fighter he is, held firm. Despite what the pundits had predicted, China's economy ended up taking the biggest hit. Its retaliatory tariffs, which would have scared away a lesser president, did not daunt President Trump. Instead, he went on the attack. Whenever China's propaganda machine advanced some grand proclamation, he'd call their bluff time and time again. On August 20, 2018, the president announced dramatic increases in tariffs on goods imported from China and tweeted that China was "an enemy," suggesting that US corporations should find other places to do business.

As he expected, China caved. On January 15, 2020, as China hid the coronavirus from the world, President Trump sat with Vice Premier Liu He at the White House and signed what he called "Phase 1" of a new trade deal. Stepping up to the microphone after the truce was signed, the president said, "We mark more than just an agreement; we mark a sea change in international trade. At long last, Americans have a government that puts them first."

At the time, it was a great victory—the beginning of a new age. None of us knew the coronavirus would soon put all this progress on hold. What we know now, more than ever, is that Communist China is not our friend and cannot be believed— no matter what. But beyond the universal mistrust of China's leadership and intentions, something more important for the future of the United States has come out of this event. The political class, willfully ignorant for generations, is now starting to embrace the idea that Donald J. Trump was right: our supply chains and factories need to come home.

★

On trade, on immigration, on foreign policy, we are going to put America first again. We are going to make America wealthy again.

—President Trump, speech in Monessen,
Pennsylvania, June 28, 2016

★

CHAPTER EIGHT

THE ART OF THE TRADE DEAL

I f you read *Let Trump Be Trump*, you know that during the 2016 campaign, Donald Trump did more events than any candidate in the history of presidential politics. While Hillary Clinton was collapsing onto sidewalks or bleach-biting her email servers clean for the third or fourth time, candidate Trump was always out looking for the next stage, the next group of hands to shake, the next record-breaking crowd. It got so wild toward the end that many staff members in their midtwenties were falling over from exhaustion, begging for a quick breather, while the boss ran like hell to give his sixth speech of the day.

One afternoon in June, after a long morning of packed-to-capacity events on the East Coast, the campaign motorcade rolled into a small town in Pennsylvania called Monessen, where we'd planned one of the biggest policy speeches of the campaign. By that point, candidate Trump had already proven he could energize a crowd. Everyone knew he could speak in broad strokes about the issues that mattered to people. That was how he had defeated sixteen of the most well-funded establishment-backed Republican candidates in the history of electoral politics.

But this was the general election, and it was time to start talking about the issues with a little more depth and nuance. Remember: it was a time when most of the country—even the most die-hard supporters of the "Make America Great Again" movement—were still having a hard time imagining Donald Trump, a consummate street fighter who could outdebate anyone in the game, being sworn in by Chief Justice John Roberts on inauguration day. They knew he had the attitude, but they didn't yet know if he had the plans to back it up.

Yeah, right.

So, to project an air of professionalism and readiness, Jared Kushner came up with a plan. Working with the campaign, he decided to have Mr. Trump give a series of methodical, highly detailed speeches on his plans for the first term. The speeches would cover subjects such as trade, the military, and building the wall, and they'd be given in specially chosen locations around the country. In essence, they would be long, detailed promises to the American people—things that we could look back on in four years to assess whether President Trump had done what he'd said he would do during his first term. Now that we're there and the election of 2020 is almost upon us, we think his record looks pretty good.

Of course, you can decide for yourself.

PROMISES MADE...

By the time Trump and the team pulled into Monessen, it was around three in the afternoon. There was a big crowd of workers and their families waiting for him, and the local news media were just setting up their cameras. In front of the Alumisource building in the middle of town, the advance team had set up a wall made of old tires, aluminum cans, and twisted metal, which was meant to evoke the town's past as a major producer of steel and fuel. It was a backdrop that would leave the media talking for days.

Just like everything Trump did, the speech was about the impact of the image as much as it was about the message. In a campaign, we call it "optics," and President Trump understands that better than anyone. The advance team had also passed out copies of the speech Mr. Trump was going to be giving that day, which focused on trade deals and tariffs. To make things easy for the reporters on the trail, we made sure that each printout was fully sourced and annotated with 128 footnotes.

As he stepped up to the podium, Mr. Trump greeted the steelworkers who'd gathered in the parking lot to hear him speak. He pointed out that the location they were standing in was only thirty miles from Pittsburgh, a city that "played a central role in building our nation." There was a huge round of applause, and Mr. Trump looked down—for one of the first times ever during the campaign—at the paper in front of him, where he'd made a few notes on his copy of the address. Then he got into the meat of the speech, outlining the unfair trade deals that had led us to that point and finally making a promise to fix them.

"The legacy of Pennsylvania steelworkers lives in the bridges, railways and skyscrapers that make up our great American landscape," he said, reading from a section of the speech he had reviewed with Stephen Miller a few days before. "But our workers' loyalty was repaid with betrayal. Our politicians have aggressively pursued a policy of globalization—moving our jobs, our wealth and our factories to Mexico and overseas. Globalization has made the financial elite who donate to politicians very wealthy. But it has left millions of our workers with nothing but poverty and heartache."

All you had to do was take one look around town, and those words came alive. Driving in on the highway from Pittsburgh into Monessen was like slipping into an alternate dimension. It was a place where the American dream had been dead for years and there was almost no hope of getting it back. It seemed that wherever you looked, there were broken-down houses and empty, boarded-up storefronts. The roads into and out of town were lined with rusted-out factories, shuttered mine shafts, and the hulks of refineries that hadn't been fully operational in decades. When President Trump mentioned "American Carnage" a few months later in his inaugural address, these were the places he had in mind.

AMERICAN CARNAGE

There were wonderful people in Monessen, of course, and there still are. We know the president enjoyed meeting a few of them before his speech. But it was clear that this town, like so many others in the United States, was in deep trouble. It was long past time that someone finally listened to their residents.

It hadn't always been that way.

For decades, small towns like Monessen had thrived. Their factories had supplied the world with millions of tons of steel every year, and their refineries helped turn coal from the ground into oil and coke, which were then sold all around the country and the world. We're talking about coke as in the *fuel*, by the way, not the stuff Hunter Biden used to enjoy when he was in the navy. Throughout the 1970s and '80s, the demand for those products was so high that coal mines and steel refineries of western Pennsylvania could support hundreds of thousands of people as well as their families. On the salaries they earned working in the refineries, the people of Pennsylvania bought houses and cars and goods. They invested in small businesses around their homes. They achieved the American dream and had the full support of their government while they did it.

Then, in the mid-1980s, the process of globalization began. The federal government stepped in and started cutting deals with countries all over the world, removing the incentives for companies to buy from refineries in the United States. As we tried to create a global economy, removing tariffs on the things we imported from other countries, American goods like the ones we'd used to make in Pennsylvania, Ohio, and upstate New York became too expensive to compete on the world market. That was because countries like China and Mexico could afford to pay workers pennies for doing the same work that Americans had been doing for decades and nobody ever called them out on it. In those days, all we cared about was bringing other countries into the fold and creating a utopian "global economy"; nobody ever stopped to think about the damage we were doing to the small towns and cities of the United States in the process.

It all culminated in 1994 when President Bill Clinton signed the North American Free Trade Agreement (NAFTA). The agreement was supposed to encourage global cooperation, making it easier for the United States, Canada, and Mexico to trade goods back and forth. It eliminated the tariffs on steel so Mexico could flood the US market with its own steel. But instead of creating wealth and prosperity for all countries involved, the agreement mostly benefited Mexico and Canada, leaving the United States to writhe in the dust. It sucked the manufacturing lifeblood out of the United States and allowed Mexico to become a global powerhouse of production, which isn't surprising when you consider the fact that in those days, the average Mexican factory was paying its workers less than three dollars an hour for their labor. Mexican factories could compete because, unlike American ones, they didn't care about paying their workers a living wage, not unlike China today. We have always said that the American worker can compete with any in the world, but we need to have a level playing field; after that agreement was signed, the playing field was anything but level.

In the steel towns of Pennsylvania and Ohio, the agreement came as a real gut punch. All over the Rust Belt and the manufacturing sectors of Appalachia—particularly in states such as West Virginia, Missouri, and Georgia—factories closed, mills collapsed, and the hundreds of thousands of businesses that were supported by those giant institutions were forced to shut their doors. You couldn't run a diner on Main Street in Monessen, for instance, if there weren't a few hundred millworkers who were hungry for lunch every day. You couldn't run a grocery store out in the suburbs if the families of those workers had no money to spend.

The collapse that occurred in the wake of NAFTA was like nothing we had ever seen in the United States. But because it was happening in the small towns in the middle of the country and because it was happening to people who were mostly white and working class, nobody seemed to pay attention. Thanks to the Democrats and their obsession with identity politics, the mainstream assumptions began to be that if you were white and living in the United States, things were going just fine; you had what the liberal left determined to be "white privilege," and your whole life was fine. Any problems you had weren't even real problems, especially as far as the liberal media were concerned.

So the news networks and newspapers, always happy to throw Bill Clinton a win, maintained for years that although there were "some downsides to NAFTA"—this is the *New York Times* that we're quoting—it had been "largely good for the United States." The *Washington Post* claimed that President Trump was "making false or misleading statements about how bad the impact of NAFTA was on the United States." From their perspective, it was true; no elite journalists had beeen adversely affected.

In the wake of the devastation caused by NAFTA, plenty of people just packed up and moved away from Monessen. Between the years 1975 and 2016, when Donald Trump rolled into town, the town's population plummeted from 15,216 to just 7,277. These people left behind foreclosed businesses, empty churches, and more homes for sale than anyone was willing to buy. When they arrived in whatever towns they moved to, they were told to get an education, learn to use computers, and not be "low skilled."

By the time the 2016 election came around, only around 30 percent of adult men in Monessen were working more than twenty hours a week, mostly at the same factories and mills where their fathers and grandfathers had worked. But because we had allowed Mexico and China to produce the same products at much lower prices, the wages they earned working at those factories were pitiful—certainly not enough to support a family or buy a decent home. They were eating at fast-food restaurants and buying cheap groceries with massive sugar content. In some cases, they got hooked on opioid painkillers, which left them vulnerable to harder drugs such as heroin once the prescriptions ran out. By the time anyone in the liberal media noticed that fact, it was already far too late.

Now, that might sound a little morbid, but we think it's necessary. For too long, politicians have been writing off the devastation that was caused when Bill Clinton signed over the soul of American manufacturing to Mexico and the bureaucrats at the World Trade Organization. They've treated the devastation that's occurred in those cities and towns—what President Trump would later call "American Carnage"—as the simple cost of doing business. To them, it was all just collateral damage that happens when you're trying to create a vibrant global economy.

Even today, when the media *do* actually write a story or two about those cities and towns, it's always done with a sly, condescending tone, as if the collapse of American industry was actually the fault of the workers, not the government's. The media tend to demean and disparage the people who live and work in those communities and pejoratively call them "Trump counties."

During the campaign of 2016, newspapers used anodyne phrases such as "economic anxiety" or "working-class blues." They assumed that if a person was poor and voting for Donald Trump, it was either because (a) they weren't lucky enough to have been born in Washington, DC, or New York City, where there are plenty of jobs to have and grocery stores and shiny office buildings to work in or (b) because they were too stupid to be rich. "Low-skilled" workers who couldn't stop "longing for an era that's gone"—that's all the media saw.

When Hillary Clinton spoke to these people, she gave them the same line of left-wing propaganda that the Democrats had been spewing for years. On the rare occasion that she actually stepped into a town like Monessen, she always admitted that her husband had made one of the biggest mistakes in the history of our country when he signed NAFTA. Then, as soon as she went to speak to another audience, she'd call the Trans-Pacific Partnership (TPP), which was pretty much just NAFTA with Asian countries, "the gold standard" of trade deals.

As Joe Biden makes his way across the Rust Belt this fall, expect nothing less from him. He will tell crowds that he grew up with coal miners and understands the working class, but he really left the town he was born in when he was ten years old and has lived in Delaware and Washington, DC, for the past sixty-seven years. At some point, you can't continue to claim to be from a place when you haven't lived there in almost seven decades.

Donald Trump, on the other hand, has never deviated from his "America First" ideas on trade. He has been saying exactly the same things for nearly four decades, and he was often the only one saying them. Back in 1999, he appeared on *Larry King Live*. When the conversation circled around to politics, he let loose. "I am [an opponent of NAFTA]," he said. "And the reason NAFTA looks OK now is because the economy is strong, but when the economy is not strong, which, unfortunately, will at some point happen, NAFTA is going to look like a disaster. . . . I'm not an isolationist. What I am, though, is I think that you have to be treated fairly by other countries. If other countries are not going to treat you fairly, Larry, I think that those countries should be—they should suffer the consequences."

A years earlier, he spoke about the same issues with Oprah Winfrey: "I don't know how your audience feels, but I think people are tired of seeing the United States ripped off. And I can't promise you everything, but I can tell you one thing: this country would make one hell of a lot of money from those people that for twenty-five years have taken advantage. It wouldn't be the way it's been, believe me. . . . If you ever go to Japan right now and try to sell something, forget about it, Oprah. Just forget about it. They come over here, they sell their cars, their VCRs, they knock the hell out of our companies."

In 1987, Trump took out a full-page ad in the *New York Times* that read, "For decades, Japan and other nations have been taking advantage of the United States. . . . It's time for us to end our vast deficits by making Japan, and others who can afford it, pay."

In 1988, on David Letterman's show, he said this: "We are living in very precarious times. If you look at what certain countries are doing to this country, such as Japan. I mean, they've totally taken advantage of the country. . . . I'm talking about the [trade] deficits. They come and they talk about free trade. They dump the cars and the VCRs and everything else. We defend Japan for virtually nothing, which is hard to believe. So when I see all that, I get very nervous, but I think George Bush is going to do a great job, and he's going to straighten—hopefully—he'll straighten it out."

A decade later, in 1999, Donald Trump even thought about running for president as a candidate for the Reform Party, which was founded by Ross Perot on a single issue: repealing NAFTA. When he officially changed his party affiliation to the Independence Party (which was New York's version of the

Reform Party), Trump told the press, "I understand this stuff. I understand good times and I understand bad times. I mean, why is a politician going to do a better job than I am?"

Want some more?

Way back in 1987, when President Ronald Reagan was debating NAFTA, Donald Trump was invited to speak at the Rotary Club in Portsmouth, New Hampshire, by a guy named Mike Dunbar, who'd launched a "Draft Trump" campaign. Although he never said he was a candidate for president during that speech, Mr. Trump lit up the room that afternoon. If there had been a roof on the place—the event was held outside—he would have blown it off.

"There is a way you can ask them," he said, talking about Japan and other countries we'd been trading with, "and they will give it, if you have the right person asking. I'm tired of nice people already in Washington. I want someone who is tough and knows how to negotiate. If not, our country faces disaster."

Well, it would take nearly forty years, but we finally found our tough guy.

Actually, almost twenty-seven years later, speaking just a few miles from the Rotary Club at the 2014 Citizens United Freedom Summit in Manchester, New Hampshire, Donald Trump stayed on message. You might notice how little things have changed. In politics, that kind of consistency is extremely rare.

"I'm a big believer in free trade," he said. "But you know, with free trade, you need competent people. I actually don't like free trade with incompetent people because everybody is kicking our ass. Every country! So I like to say fair trade as opposed to free trade. I like to say smart trade which I haven't heard, but I've come up with it very recently. Very smart trade. As you know, I know people on Wall Street . . . that if I put them to negotiate against China, Japan, Mexico, you name them. I mean, I could go on forever because we have no good deals anymore."

We could go on, but you probably get the point. If you'd like to try this little exercise yourself, just go ahead and type "Donald Trump NAFTA free trade" into Google. You'll find some of Hillary Clinton's lost emails before you find a single instance of the boss contradicting himself.

All throughout the campaign of 2016, Donald Trump carried that message. He crafted his message in the early primary states of New Hampshire, Iowa, and South Carolina, and then, when the message was perfect and the country was ready to hear it, he went wide, out to places like Monessen, Pennsylvania; Morgantown, West Virginia; and Grand Rapids, Michigan, that were really feeling the pain. Unlike other politicians, who change their positions like the wind, Donald Trump had never wavered on this point. Maybe that's why when he finished his speech in Monessen with a promise to repeal NAFTA and bring jobs back to the United States, they actually believed him. Pennsylvania, as you probably know, voted for Mr. Trump in 2016, and the congressional district that includes Monessen voted for him with 58 percent of the vote.

At the end of his speech, Donald Trump made seven promises, each of which represented seismic shifts in the foreign policy of the United States. Because this section of the book is about how well President Trump has kept his promises, we figured we would list them right here for reference. As you keep reading, please keep in mind these promises, which he made during his jobs plan speech in Monessen in June 2016. See if you can find a single one that he's failed to live up to.

One: I am going to withdraw the United States from the Trans-Pacific Partnership, which has not yet been ratified.

Two: I'm going to appoint the toughest and smartest trade negotiators to fight on behalf of American workers.

Three: I'm going to direct the Secretary of Commerce to identify every violation of trade agreements a foreign country is currently using to harm our workers. I will then direct all appropriate agencies to use every tool under American and international law to end these abuses.

Four: I'm going to tell our NAFTA partners that I intend to immediately renegotiate the terms of that agreement to get a better deal for our workers. And I don't mean just a little bit better, I mean a lot better. If they do not agree to a renegotiation, then I will submit notice under Article 2205 of the NAFTA agreement that America intends to withdraw from the deal.

Five: I am going to instruct my Treasury Secretary to label China a currency manipulator. Any country that devalues their currency in order to take advantage of the United States will be met with sharply.

Six: I am going to instruct the U.S. Trade Representative to bring trade cases against China, both in this country and at the WTO. China's unfair subsidy behavior is prohibited by the terms of its entrance to the WTO, and I intend to enforce those rules.

Seven: If China does not stop its illegal activities, including its theft of American trade secrets, I will use every lawful presidential power to remedy trade disputes, including the application of tariffs consistent with Section 201 and 301 of the Trade Act of 1974 and Section 232 of the Trade Expansion Act of 1962.

As you know from the last chapter, President Trump made good on promises five, six, and seven almost as soon as he got into office. He labeled China a currency manipulator—an almost unprecedented move in the modern era—and worked with his trade team to slap some massive tariffs on them, eventually winning a trade war that nobody believed was possible.

Of course, as he was listing those promises from the podium in Monessen, Donald Trump must have known how hard it was going to be to keep them. He knew as well as anyone that once a president actually gets into the White House, political forces can take hold and stop an administration's agenda before it even gets off the ground.

Almost as soon as he stepped into the White House President Trump was besieged on all sides by enemies—people from the farthest corners of the establishment who didn't want his "America First" agenda to succeed. The story of how he beat those people, found the right allies within the building, and managed to keep his promises despite unprecedented obstacles is the *real* story of the Trump presidency.

THE SWAMP STRIKES BACK

On the one hundredth day of President Trump's first term, things were looking good—at least from the outside. The president had begun laying the groundwork for implementing tariffs under the law, letting countries such as China and

India know that if they did not reform their trade practices soon, our economic retribution would be swift and painful. He had also withdrawn the United States from the Trans-Pacific Partnership before it could even be signed, avoiding the disastrous consequences that would have come when the deal went into full effect. (For those of you keeping score at home, that's promise number one in the can, putting him at four out of seven.)

Because of the pressure coming from the White House, companies from all over the world had begun investing in the United States again. In January, just a few days before President Trump was inaugurated, General Motors began the process of bringing thousands of IT jobs back into the United States, creating a total of seven thousand new jobs and investing just over $1 billion. Ford Motor Company, a company President Trump had attacked repeatedly on the campaign trail for its tendency to build cheap cars in Mexico rather than the United States, announced that it was canceling plans to build two new manufacturing plants south of the border.

In a tweet on January 4, he thanked them:

Thank you to Ford for scrapping a new plant in Mexico and creating 7,000 new jobs in the U.S. This is just the beginning—much more to follow
         —@realDonaldTrump, January 4, 2017

In September 2016, an opportunity to visit the Flint, Michigan, water treatment facility presented itself. The people of Flint were suffering from undrinkable tap water and were looking for help. Dave recognized the importance of the issue immediately and scheduled Mr. Trump to give a speech in Flint. When he spoke directly to the people of Michigan, he uttered these famous words: "It used to be, cars were made in Flint and you couldn't drink the water in Mexico. Now, the cars are made in Mexico and you cannot drink the water in Flint. That's not good. We shouldn't allow it to happen. They'll [Ford] make their cars, they'll employ thousands and thousands of people, not from this country . . . and we'll have nothing but more unemployment in Flint." It was a seminal speech and may have helped deliver Michigan to the win column six weeks later.

––––––––––––

As usual, he was right on the money. During the president's first hundred days in office, hundreds of thousands of new jobs poured back into the United States. Walmart added ten thousand new jobs when they built new offices in the United States, and they agreed to purchase $250 billion more of American-made, -grown, and -assembled products through 2023.

From there, though, his accomplishments stalled. Despite getting more done in its first hundred days than any other administration in history, the Trump administration was still lagging on a few key issues—things that should have been easy in a normal, well-staffed administration. President Trump's promise to pull the United States out of NAFTA, for instance, was still stalled in the bureaucracy and red tape of the West Wing. What should have been done with a single signed letter from the president had taken months, and nobody was quite sure why.

There was a problem somewhere, and the president wanted to find out what it was.

So on his ninety-seventh day in the White House, April 25, 2017, President Trump called a meeting in the Oval Office to talk about trade. He wanted to get an update on the promises he'd made during the campaign because his hundredth day in office was approaching. In the Oval Office that day were Vice President Mike Pence, Commerce Secretary Wilbur Ross, Senior Advisor Jared Kushner, Peter Navarro, the president's expert on tariffs and trade, and Rob Porter, the staff secretary in the West Wing. Gary Cohn, the former executive from Goldman Sachs who'd been fighting the president's "America First" agenda since day one, was not invited to the meeting.

Toward the end of the meeting, President Trump mentioned NAFTA, pointing out that it had been nearly one hundred days since he took office and the withdrawal still hadn't occurred. He demanded that someone bring him the proper documentation so he could announce it during the address he was planning to give on his one hundredth day in office. It was a direct order from the commander in chief, and it was impossible to misunderstand.

"I want it on my desk Friday," he said.

In front of the desk, Rob Porter got worried. According to someone who was present at the meeting, he stammered through an explanation, trying to convince the president it was too soon. He said that before the United States could withdraw from NAFTA, someone in the West Wing would need to draw up a detailed plan to *replace* NAFTA. He said that it would probably be better if we "did this in the proper order" and "thought it through."

Now, if you're aware of Rob Porter's history, you probably know that he was not against the deal because he thought things were moving too fast or because he wanted to make sure it was done through the proper channels. Many have said he was trying to slow roll the deal because he didn't want it to get done in the first place. He, along with several others in the Trump administration, had seemingly been fighting against the president's "America First" agenda from day one, and their deceit was just beginning to show itself.

Since their first days in the West Wing, Rob Porter, Gary Cohn, and other globalists in the Trump White House had had an alternative agenda to that of the president. They were classic big-government elite Swamp creatures who didn't want President Trump to upend the traditional power structures of Washington the way he'd promised to do during the campaign. So they worked against him from the inside.

About nine months later, after they'd both left the West Wing, they would sit down with Bob Woodward, the dean of the Washington press corps, to admit that they removed papers from the president's desk to prevent him from signing them. Woodward's book *Fear*, which exposed these two bad hombres, rocketed to the top of the *New York Times* bestseller list for its salacious material. The president expressed his outrage that the staff never told him Woodward wanted to interview him for the book. He told us he was disappointed he didn't get the chance to speak to Woodward directly.

Before those guys departed the White House, they managed to do some (very minor) damage to the president's "America First" agenda. Together, they formed something that came to be called the "Wall Street Wing," a group of dissident political forces inside the West Wing whose mission was to thwart the president's agenda from the inside. Anyone who had the ear of the president and *wasn't* a globalist establishment Republican like them was forbidden to see the boss.

When they realized that President Trump liked hearing from Peter Navarro, for example, the guy who was with the president 100 percent on tariffs and trade agreements, they tried like hell to keep him out of the Oval Office.

Still, the president managed to accomplish amazing things. As his term went on, he instilled a sense of patriotism into the country again, and he signed historic tax cuts into law that benefited working-class Americans more than anyone. Before long, he realized who was in the building to help him and who was there only to burnish their own image. On May 11, less than a month after the meeting in which he demanded a piece of paper that would get the United States out of NAFTA, the president got the secret weapon he would need to get the deal done. After a relatively contentious nomination battle, Robert Lighthizer was confirmed as the president's US trade representative. Remember when Trump had promised the crowd that he would get "the toughest and smartest trade negotiators to fight on behalf of American workers"? Lighthizer was the guy. (That's promise number two down.)

Lighthizer understood that the president had strong instincts on trade, and he knew that when President Trump trusted those instincts, the American people usually benefited. Over the next two years, he, Navarro, and Jared Kushner would work with a staff of tough negotiators to completely retool the United States' trade relationship with Mexico and Canada. On October 1, 2018, President Trump announced that he was withdrawing from the deal, saying that he would

replace it with something that would benefit American workers rather than Mexican factories.

In the Rose Garden two days later, he announced a plan
that would be called the United States–Mexico–Canada
Agreement (USMCA): "I am thrilled to speak to the American people to share truly historic news for our nation, and,
indeed, for the world. . . . It is my great honor to announce that
we have successfully completed negotiations on a brand-new
deal to replace NAFTA and the NAFTA trade agreements
with an incredible new US–Mexico–Canada Agreement,
called 'USMCA.' . . . Throughout the campaign, I promised
to renegotiate NAFTA, and today we have kept that promise. . . .The agreement will govern nearly $1.2 trillion in trade,
which makes it the biggest trade deal in the United States'
history."

That, if you're still keeping up on your scorecard, is promise number four kept. All seven of the promises he made in
his first announcement speech were delivered upon in the
first few years of his administration. That's what you get with
Donald Trump—someone who means what he says and fol-
lows through. Although essential to his agenda, trade wasn't
the only area where he promised to put America First." Some
of his biggest victories, and promises that he kept, came in the
complete retooling of the United States' foreign policy.

CHAPTER NINE

DIPLOMACY

I have determined that it is time to officially recognize
Jerusalem as the capital of Israel. I am also directing
the State Department to begin preparation to move
the American Embassy from Tel Aviv to Jerusalem...

—@realDonaldTrump, December 6, 2017

Three days before he was sworn in as our nation's forty-fifth president, Donald Trump took one last ride on Trump Force One, the modified 757 he'd taken all over the country during the campaign. It had been three months since Mr. Trump and the "misfit toys" of his campaign had pulled off the greatest political upset in American history, and the world was still reeling from the shock. All around the country, as the pundits and political hacks were waking up to the fact that yes, Donald Trump really *was* going to be the president, they started writing—a lot. They wrote about the forces that propelled Donald Trump into the White House, what he was going to do when he got there, and what his election meant for the rest of the world.

As usual, they got it all wrong.

David Remnick, writing in *The New Yorker*, wrote a piece that went viral called "An American Tragedy," saying that Trump's election was "a triumph for the forces, at home and abroad, of nativism, authoritarianism, misogyny, and racism." He wrote that the election of President Trump would "set markets tumbling" and that Donald Trump's "disdain for democratic norms" would lead to "all manner of national decline and suffering." Writing in the *New York Times*, Paul Krugman famously served up this shit sandwich of a prediction:

> It really does now look like President Donald J. Trump, and markets are plunging. When might we expect them to recover?
>
> Frankly, I find it hard to care much, even though this is my specialty. The disaster for America and the world has so many aspects that the economic ramifications are way down on my list of things to fear.
>
> Still, I guess people want an answer: If the question is when markets will recover, a first-pass answer is never.

About twenty-four hours after that column was published, the markets started to recover, and they didn't stop climbing until a once-in-a-century pandemic swept across the globe and tore the world economy to shreds. So you could say that Mr. Krugman was a little off base on that part of it. As for the rest of what he was talking about—the "ramifications" of Trump becoming president—we're not really sure. Maybe this guy is against increasing wages for our men and women in uniform or deregulating the government so small businesses can grow? Maybe he doesn't like the most robust economy in the history of the United States?

No matter what else those writers worried about, their most pressing concern was always the rest of the world. When it came down to it, all these geniuses seemed to believe that Donald Trump was completely ill equipped to deal with the demands of foreign policy. Back in those days, the Washington establishment, including Susan Rice, John Brennan, and John Kerry, was terrified that once he took office, the president would continue to conduct himself on the world stage the way he'd conducted himself on the campaign. They thought he'd keep making brash statements on the fly, talking to world leaders like a tough guy from Queens, and announcing major shifts in foreign policy via Twitter.

Admittedly, the past few months hadn't given them much to be enthusiastic about. Since the moment he won, President-elect Trump had not shifted a single inch on any of the promises he'd made during the campaign. Asked whether he was still going to build the wall, he said, "Absolutely." Pressed on whether he was still going to back out of the Paris Agreement on climate change, he said, "Yes, of course." In fact, if you went back to his first big speech on foreign policy, the actions President Trump had taken so far during the transition made perfect sense.

Much like the speech on trade he'd given in Monessen, Pennsylvania, Mr. Trump's first foreign policy speech was supposed to assure the country that he had a plan he could stick to—a road map that he'd follow for his entire first term. In it, he lobbed grenades into the traditional foreign policy establishment of Washington, DC, telling them that the way they'd been doing things for years had been a complete and total disaster—and we're not exaggerating. In fact, here's a direct quote: "Our foreign policy is a complete and total disaster. No vision. No purpose. No direction. No strategy."

Throughout the speech, which he gave on April 27, 2016, candidate Trump identified five main weaknesses in the foreign policy of the United States under Barack Obama. Take a look at them, and as you read the rest of the chapter, decide whether or not you think these are still problems we're facing after four years of President Trump.

> First, our resources are totally overextended. President Obama has weakened our military by weakening our economy.
>
> We're rebuilding other countries while weakening our own. Ending the theft of American jobs will give us the resources we need to rebuild our military, which has to happen and regain our financial independence and strength. . . .
>
> Secondly, our allies are not paying their fair share, and I've been talking about this recently a lot. Our allies must contribute toward their financial political, and human costs. . . .
>
> Thirdly, our friends are beginning to think they can't depend on us. We've had a president who dislikes our friends and bows to our enemies. . . . He negotiated a disastrous nuclear deal with Iran, and then we watched them ignore its terms before the ink was even dry. . . .
>
> Israel, our great friend and one true democracy in the Middle East has been snubbed and criticized by

an administration that lacks moral clarity. Just a few days ago, Vice President Biden again criticized Israel, a force for justice and peace, for acting as an impatient peace area in the region. . . .

Fourth, our rivals no longer respect us. In fact, they're just as confused as our allies, but an even bigger problem is they don't take us seriously anymore. The truth is they don't respect us. . . .

Finally, America no longer has a clear understanding of our foreign policy goals. Since the end of the Cold War and the breakup of the Soviet Union, we've lacked a coherent foreign policy.

Toward the middle of the speech, Mr. Trump repeated a line that had become famous in the early days of the campaign. Speaking about the weak negotiators and the Swamp creatures who have been running our country into the ground, he said, "I'm the only one—believe me, I know them all, I'm the only one who knows how to fix it."

Clearly, candidate Trump was ready to shake up the Washington foreign policy establishment—and if he had to do it all by himself, then so be it. By January 17, the night he took his final ride on Trump Force One, he had already gotten started.

On December 23, 2016, for instance, President-elect Trump ordered the State Department to send a cable to all politically appointed diplomats serving under President Obama to be back home by noon on inauguration day. This was not an unprecedented move, but it did send a message. It ensured that when Mr. Trump finally did take office on January 20, he would be in complete control of America's foreign policy.

In theory, there would be no more Deep State bureaucrats or career government officials to undermine the president's message, and there would be no more weak negotiators serving as our sole representatives in foreign countries. The truth is, President Trump would find out later that the Deep State is alive and well under his administration and doing everything it can to destroy him.

Beginning on the first day of President Trump's term, there would be nothing but the Trump Doctrine and the small group of patriots willing to work from the White House to enforce it. Any diplomats he nominated would be vetted by him personally and tested for their skills in negotiation and loyalty to the president's agenda. During the transition, a few career diplomats and foreign policy experts from the Obama administration—all of whom had been betting on a Hillary Clinton victory—told *Foreign Policy* magazine that they were "having trouble connecting with the Trump administration."

Uh, yeah. That wasn't phone trouble, guys. We'd just been hoping you'd take the hint.

Of course, it did make the event that President-elect Trump was attending that evening a little awkward. Down in the thick of the Swamp, the inaugural committee had organized something called the Chairman's Global Dinner: a black-tie, invitation-only celebration of the world's diplomats. It would be held under the sixty-foot ceiling of the Andrew W. Mellon Auditorium in Washington, DC, the go-to spot for elite Washington insiders. Throughout the evening, these diplomats would listen to music from the southern rock band Alabama, sip champagne, and dine on filet mignon or mustard glazed black cod. As the music played, foreign diplomats would walk the floor of the auditorium, meeting the new members of the Trump administration, talking strategy, and advocating for the best interests of their respective countries.

In a sense, this dinner was a celebration of everything that President Trump had come to Washington to destroy. For decades, foreign policy had been decided by low-level diplomats like the ones who gathered in the Mellon Auditorium that evening. When the United States made deals, it was those people who'd sit in rooms for hours—sometimes days and weeks—trying to hammer out the details. Miraculously, they always found a way to change absolutely nothing. President Obama had given them broad leeway to negotiate, and obviously, it hadn't worked out. They'd given us NAFTA, the Paris Agreement, and the Iran deal—all of which served to weaken the United States abroad. It's because of them that our allies—as President Trump pointed out in problem number three above—didn't think they could rely on us. It's also their fault that our enemies—as President Trump pointed out in point number four—didn't respect us.

Those people weren't chosen because they were the best or because they had negotiated good deals in the past; they were chosen because they had served the most time, donated to the right political candidates, or knew the right people in Washington. They were hired based on their connections in the Beltway and promoted based on how well they followed the rules. Worst of all, they were beholden to the people who helped them get their jobs, not the American people.

When President Trump took office, he had promised to completely annihilate this way of doing business, and most of the people who'd assembled that evening knew it. Already he had promised to ban all former White House officials from becoming lobbyists for at least five years. He would send a message to the world that the United States was under new management and that all orders came directly from the top.

When President-elect Trump came through the curtains of the auditorium and grabbed the microphone from Vice President–elect Mike Pence, he was as kind and jovial as ever. Every head in the room turned to look at him, and the whole place fell silent.

President-elect Trump commented on the music, the food, the lights, and the inauguration ceremonies that would take place in a few days. Then he made a joke about a group called Bikers for Trump that had come down to Washington in droves to witness the president's inauguration. As you probably know, there is nothing President Trump likes more than hanging out with people who are *not* from Washington. Given the choice between dining on filet mignon with the diplomats and going out for a burger with the Bikers for Trump, you'd better believe he'll take the burger every time.

Referring to the selection of Mike Pence as his running mate, Mr. Trump said, "I had a couple of beauties I could have picked. They were good too but maybe wouldn't have worked out like Mike." It was true. During the campaign, Corey served as the chairman of the vice presidential selection committee and was intimately involved with the selection of what many have said was the president's best decision, Mike Pence. Vice President Pence is a great partner of President Trump inside the White House and did a fantastic job when it became his duty to chair the government's response to the coronavirus.

Toward the end of his remarks, Trump found Rex Tillerson, a former CEO of ExxonMobil and the president's choice to be the next secretary of state, in the crowd and pointed him out. He said Rex would do a good job, then made a small joke at his expense: "He's led this charmed life. He goes to one country, takes the oil, goes into another country. It's tough dealing with these politicians, right?"

President-elect Trump was joking that night, of course. But in the months to come, he would end up being exactly right about Rex Tillerson. When it came time to implement President Trump's agenda—backing out of the Iran deal, making our allies in NATO pay up—Tillerson would side with Gary Cohn, James Mattis, and other globalists in the Trump White House every time. He would join them in slow rolling the president's agenda, refusing direct orders, and leaking damaging information to the press to hurt the Trump agenda. It's no wonder he was fired while on the toilet a little over a year into the job.

As he predicted during the campaign, President Trump would have to go it alone for most of his first term. Considering that, the amazing things he was able to achieve are even more impressive. In a show of how much he cared for the pomp and circumstance of inaugural celebrations, the president-elect left the Mellon Auditorium right after giving that short speech, leaving the diplomats high and dry, so he could go spend one more night in his longtime home of New York City.

As he was leaving, President-elect Trump stopped to talk with a reporter from an Israeli newspaper called *Israel Hayom*.

Speaking in broken English, the reporter asked the president-elect whether he had "not forgotten [his] promise con-
cerning the embassy in Jerusalem."

It was a good question. During the campaign, President
Trump had repeatedly promised that if he won the presidency, he would move the US Embassy from Tel Aviv to Jerusalem, effectively recognizing that Jerusalem was the capital
of Israel, not Palestine. This was a major shift in the foreign
policy of the United States.

It was also a promise that every presidential candidate
since George H. W. Bush had made. In terms of foreign policy, it was like a great white whale. Every president knew that
moving the embassy could have major consequences in the
peace process between Israel and Palestine. This is because
both Palestinians and Israelis claimed Jerusalem as their capital; they'd been fighting over the city for decades. Typically,
the United States liked to say it was on the side of Israel, but
during the eight years of the Obama administration, rarely
did anything to show that to the world.

After Bill Clinton won the White House in 1992, he criticized George H. W. Bush for not keeping his promise to move
the embassy. Then, in 1993, after he signed the Oslo Accords,
which kicked off a new era in the peace process between
Israelis and Palestinians, he gave up on moving the embassy
because he didn't want to upset anyone. In 2000, George
W. Bush criticized Bill Clinton for not moving the embassy
but then failed to do it during his eight years in office, again
because he didn't want to offend anyone. When Barack
Obama ran for president in 2008, it was the same story; he
said that "Jerusalem will remain the capital of Israel, and

it must remain undivided." Then he walked it back almost immediately, saying "Well, obviously, it's going to be up to the parties to negotiate a range of these issues. And Jerusalem will be part of those negotiations." By the end of his presidency, Barack Obama had also failed to move the embassy to Jerusalem.

President-elect Trump, on the other hand, wasn't backing down. "Yes," he said, looking the reporter in the eye, "we're still going to move the embassy."

Before leaving the building, the president turned back around. "You know," he said. "I am not someone who breaks promises."

THE CHOSEN ONE

The next morning, January 18, Barack Obama took to the podium in the White House Press Briefing Room one last time before he packed up his desk and hit the road for good. For the press, it was a sad day. They had been covering the Obama administration for eight blissful years, always happy to swallow the talking points of the day, attend fancy parties, and write puff pieces about the staff.

That era, they knew, was coming to an end. President Trump had already declared war on the Fake News, and he was coming into the White House ready for battle. Even then, the reporters in the room had no idea what was coming.

Toward the middle of the briefing, one of the reporters in the room—obviously reacting to the promise President Trump had repeated the night before—asked Barack Obama's opinion on moving the embassy to Jerusalem and then about the Israeli-Palestinian conflict more generally. After taking a *big*

breath, the now former president launched into this nonsensi-
cal word salad of an answer. (Strap in.)

> I'm worried about it both because I think the status
> quo is unsustainable, that it is dangerous for Israel,
> that it is bad for Palestinians, it is bad for the region,
> and it is bad for America's national security.
>
> And I came into this office wanting to do every-
> thing I could to encourage serious peace talks between
> Israelis and Palestinians. And we invested a lot of
> energy, a lot of time, a lot of effort, first year, second
> year, all the way until last year. Ultimately, what has
> always been clear is that we cannot force the parties to
> arrive at peace. What we can do is facilitate, provide a
> platform, encourage. But we can't force them to do it.
>
> But in light of shifts in Israeli politics and Pales-
> tinian politics; a rightward drift in Israeli politics; a
> weakening of President Abbas's ability to move and
> take risks on behalf of the Palestinian Territories;
> in light of all the dangers that have emerged in the
> region . . .
>
> I don't see how this issue gets resolved in a way
> that maintains Israel as both Jewish and a democracy,
> because if you do not have two states, then in some
> form or fashion you are extending an occupation,
> functionally you end up having one state in which
> millions of people are disenfranchised and operate as
> second-class occupant-residents. . . .
>
> So the President-elect will have his own policy.
> The ambassador—or the candidate for the ambassa-
> dorship obviously has very different views than I do.

. . . I think my views are clear. We'll see how their approach plays itself out.

I don't want to project today what could end up happening, but obviously it's a volatile environment.

But if you're going to make big shifts in policy, just make sure you've thought it through . . . you want to be intentional about it. You don't want to do things off the cuff when it comes to an issue this volatile.

You didn't actually read that whole thing, did you? Good.

Look, when you've been in politics as long as we have, you have to hear a lot of answers like that. In fact, if you spend any time in Washington at all, you'll get the chance to hear a lot of people—mostly Democrats—speak for hours and hours while saying absolutely nothing at all.

It's an amazing thing to see, really.

These people will use phrases such as "Mistakes were made" and "We'll look into that" and "Well, you know, it's a complicated issue," all to cover up the fact that they can't take a position on anything. With so many political advisors and pundits and speechwriters weighing in from all sides of the building, actually getting anything done can seem impossible. In the quote above, you can see that Barack Obama did absolutely nothing to address the crisis in the Middle East during his eight years in office, talking and talking and talking (and talking and talking) about why he had repeatedly failed to address a problem that during the campaign he had sworn he could fix. Looking back, it's almost as though he was trying to run out the clock before the bell rang. Tellingly, there was no follow-up question from the reporter. The press was happy to take everything that Obama had to say and regurgitate it with smiles on their faces.

Corey remembers sitting backstage when candidate Trump said President Obama had made our friends think they can't depend on us during his first foreign policy speech in April 2016. This was exactly the kind of nonsense he was talking about. During the eight years Obama was in the White House, his administration said over and over again that Israel was our ally. They knew that Israel expected, and deserved, our protection and friendship. We had agreed to give it to them repeatedly.

Yet when Obama, then the commander in chief, was asked about how to defend Israel, he talked for a full four minutes without saying anything at all. It was as though he distilled his administration's views on Israel down into one boring, barely comprehensible speech.

Throughout his administration, Barack Obama relied on diplomats, ambassadors, and low-level staffers to try to solve one of the greatest problems the world has ever known. They made policy from the basement of the West Wing, slow rolled key goals, and seemed to care about getting things done only during election years.

He also relied on them to negotiate the Iran nuclear deal, which ended up being an absolute disaster for the United States and our allies. All along, Iran has considered Israel its greatest enemy, and we negotiated with it. As part of the deal, the Obama administration sent Iran $1.74 billion in cash on pallets—clearly, the negotiators from that night at the Mellon were very good at their jobs. (On May 8, 2018, President Trump would officially withdraw the United States from that disastrous agreement—but we're getting ahead of ourselves.)

Much as their boss would do during his final press conference, the members of the Obama-Biden administration would talk and talk for hours about the problem. They'd organize study groups and poll tests and try to figure out how the moves they were making would appear to the public. The only time any of them ever took action was to order lunch or set up another meeting.

Together, we believe, they formed the single most ineffective administration in the history of this country, and we all paid the price for it.

———

President Trump, on the other hand, got started right away. When he took office, he took a hard look at a law that Congress had passed in 1995 that required the United States to move the embassy. Under the terms of the law, which was called the Jerusalem Embassy Act, the president of the United States had to sign a waiver every time he didn't move the embassy. Since the law was passed, approximately forty waivers had been signed, kicking the can down the road for more than twenty years.

Fortunately for President Trump, the law meant that actually moving the embassy would be easy. All he had to do was *not* sign the waiver, and the process could begin. Of course, he put some of the best minds in the White House onto the case. He put Jared Kushner in charge of overseeing a small team, and together they made plans to move the embassy.

On May 14, 2018, it finally opened, and the whole country of Israel was ecstatic.

About eighteen months later, Corey got a call from Aaron Klein, a reporter from Breitbart who works in Israel. Klein knew that Benjamin Netanyahu, the prime minister of Israel, was having trouble with his reelection campaign. Of course, "trouble" wasn't the right word; it's probably more accurate to say that Netanyahu, who was running for his fifth term as prime minister, had absolutely no campaign infrastructure behind him. He had no team, no office, and no strategy to win reelection.

A few days later, we were on a plane to Israel.

If the campaign of 2016 taught us anything, it's how to mobilize a base, sell a candidate to the people, and mow down the electoral competition. So just a few hours after we touched down in Israel, that's exactly what we did. Using as our home base a conference room at the Leonardo Plaza hotel, which was close to the new embassy in Jerusalem, we put together a winning strategy for Netanyahu. We brought in experts from the Trump campaign like Tony Fabrizio to join John McLaughlin on the polling team, Susie Wiles, Matt Palumbo, and Jay Connaughton. We also took a look at what Netanyahu's team was already doing and came up with a plan to fix it.

In those days, for example, Prime Minister Netanyahu would come out onstage during his rallies with a few dozen other people, then defer to them as he spoke. Clearly, that wasn't going to do it. We suggested that instead, he go more in the Trump direction: a bare stage, loud music, and as much energy as he could muster. The next time he did a rally, he took our recommendations. He was the only one onstage, had energetic supporters behind him, and walked out to the thumping beat of "Eye of the Tiger." Much better! And of course, he went on to win!

The Jerusalem embassy is a perfect example of foreign policy in the age of Trump. It was a bold move that no other president would have made, and to this day, the apocalyptic consequences everyone warned President Trump about have not come to pass. As Jared Kushner said on the day the embassy first opened, the move was "a prelude to peace, not the end of it."

Between the day he was inaugurated and the day he moved the Jerusalem embassy, President Trump experienced plenty of unprecedented foreign policy challenges, and he faced down every single one of them with grace, resolve, and grit.

In fact, he probably had more disasters come across his desk than any other president in recent memory. Between the withdrawal from the Iran deal, the drawdown of troops in Afghanistan, and the constant threat of nuclear war from North Korea, President Trump fought ten battles a day. And somehow, he's managed to emerge victorious from each one.

Speaking of which . . .

LITTLE ROCKET MAN

On August 26, 2017, almost exactly a year before President Trump would speak by video to thousands of jubilant worshippers in front of the new Jerusalem embassy, millions of people in northern Japan awoke with a flashing alarm on the screens of their cell phones. "A missile was fired from North Korea," it said. "Please evacuate to a sturdy building or basement."

In the middle of the night, Kim Jong-un, the supreme
leader of North Korea, had launched a ballistic missile over
the island of Hokkaido, the northernmost major island of
Japan. Nobody, including our top intelligence experts, knew
what was coming next. With Kim, it was impossible to tell. For
more than eight years, this crazy little man had been threatening to launch missiles or conduct nuclear tests in order to
assert his country's power on the world stage. He knew, as a
tyrant overseeing a dysfunctional country, that the only way
to stay in power was to threaten to blow the world up at any
moment. Without that, no other country would have reason
to fear him or, at the very least, negotiate with him. For Kim
Jong-un, this missile test was just another flailing effort to
assert power on the world stage.

If he'd done it just one year earlier, it might have worked.

When Barack Obama was in charge, such displays of
aggression had always been treated as grave threats. That was
why they kept working. In 2009, when Kim Jong-un's father,
Kim Jong-il, launched missiles, President Obama tried to set
up a meeting with the regime but was rebuffed over and over
again. If Obama had still been in charge when Kim Jong-un
initiated his latest rocket test, things would have stayed
largely the same. There would have been meetings, drafts of
speeches, and finally some kind of weak televised address by
the president, warning that the United States wouldn't stand
for any sign of aggression against our allies. He would have
used words such as "unacceptable" or "dangerous," and we
all would have waited around to see what happened. Perhaps
a strongly worded letter would have followed.

With Donald Trump behind the Resolute Desk, though,
things played out a little differently. He didn't contact a

diplomat or call the State Department to see when he could set up a conference call with Kim Jong-un to say "Please, sir, could you stop threatening the world?" He didn't even think twice. Instead, he did what he'd been doing for nearly five decades in the boardroom: he saw the problem, weighed his options, and then came at his adversary with the full force of a Gulf Coast hurricane.

Minutes after learning about the launch, President Trump attended a scheduled meeting on the opioid crisis. Toward the end of his remarks, after a reporter asked him about his position on Kim Jong-un and the recent missile test he'd just initiated, he went off script, as he had so many times during the 2016 campaign. Such times, as you probably know, are when all the good stuff comes out.

"North Korea best not make any more threats to the United States," he said. "They will be met with fire and fury like the world has never seen. . . . He has been very threatening beyond a normal state, and as I said, they will be met with fire and fury, and frankly power the likes of which this world has never seen before."

It's hard to overstate just how shocking it was the first time we heard this type of honesty. This was the kind of language we hadn't heard from a president of the United States since President Harry Truman, speaking from the Oval Office after the United States had dropped the first atomic bomb on Hiroshima, warned Japan of "a rain of ruin from the air, the like of which has never been seen on this earth."

After President Trump's first ultimatum, Kim Jong-un fired back, as President Trump knew he would. He called the president a "mentally deranged US dotard" and said he would "tame [him] with fire." At the time, President Trump was at the United Nations, listening to the representatives of other countries speak. One of them was the foreign minister of North Korea, who was talking about nuclear nonproliferation. Shortly after the speech, President Trump posted this on Twitter:

> Just heard foreign Minister of North Korea speak at U.N.
> If he echoes thoughts of Little Rocket Man, they won't be
> around much longer!
> —@realDonaldTrump, September 23, 2017

As anyone who's read *Let Trump Be Trump* knows, the president has always been a big Elton John fan. We're not surprised that when it came time to pick a nickname for Kim Jong-un, he called him by the title of one of the singer's biggest hits. During his own address to the United Nations, he doubled down, saying:

> The United States has great strength and patience, but if it is forced to defend itself or its allies, we will have no choice but to totally destroy North Korea. Rocket Man is on a suicide mission for himself and for his regime. The United States is ready, willing and able, but hopefully this will not be necessary. That's what the United Nations is all about; that's what the United Nations is for. Let's see how they do.

Incidentally, it was also during that speech that President Trump announced that the United States military would soon be the strongest it had ever been. Working closely with

Secretary of Defense James Mattis and Senate majority leader Mitch McConnell, he had arranged for $700 billion in new funding to the military, the most any president had ever managed to secure during a first term. Of course, nobody paid any attention to that part. During that UN General Assembly (UNGA), it was all about North Korea. When the pundits heard what President Trump had said on the subject, they went insane. His speech at the United Nations went far beyond anything Harry Truman or any other president had ever said during an address to the world.

What the pundits didn't consider, of course, was the fact that President Trump was speaking in the only language that Kim Jong-un would understand. He was meeting the crazy little man on his own terms, going right back at the brutal dictator twice as hard as Kim had come at the United States. He was implementing a strategy that would work perfectly in the months to come.

Once again, though, the president was met with resistance from within his own administration. Shortly after the president spoke at the United Nations, Rex Tillerson, speaking while on a trip to Beijing, went on television to read a statement regarding North Korea, trying out the old Obama approach of sucking up to dictators: "We ask: 'Would you like to talk?' We have lines of communication to Pyongyang." He also insisted that he and the president were "completely aligned" on their policies. But clearly, he was not on the same page.

Just a month earlier, on July 12, 2017, after a tense meeting at the Pentagon with his top military advisors, President Trump had berated Rex Tillerson for not acting quickly enough to withdraw the United States from the Iran deal. As soon as he left the room that day, Tillerson went all pouty, calling the president "a fucking moron" loud enough so everyone could hear. His remark was reported widely, as Tillerson knew it would be. By the way, if you don't like the way your face is sitting on your skull right now, go ahead and call President Trump "a fucking moron" to his face; see what happens.

That, as you can probably imagine, was the beginning of the end for Rex Tillerson. He was just one more establishment obstacle for the president to take down on his way to implementing his "America First" agenda.

In a tweet right after Tillerson made his statement, President Trump took back control but stopped short of embarrassing Tillerson in public.

> I told Rex Tillerson, our wonderful Secretary of State, that he is wasting his time trying to negotiate with Little Rocket Man...
> ...Save your energy Rex, we'll do what has to be done!
> —@realDonaldTrump, October 1, 2017

For the next few months, after things had cooled down and Kim had gotten the message, President Trump got to work once again. He fired Rex Tillerson, who was never on board with his way of doing business in the first place and brought on Mike Pompeo from his position as director of the Central Intelligence Agency. Together they worked to open real lines of communication with the North Koreans, this time from a position of power. President Trump had embarrassed the leader of their country in front of the entire world, threatening in his speech at the United Nations to blow the whole country off the face of the earth. People believed the threat. When President Trump spoke, the world didn't know if he was bluffing.

So for the first time in history, North Korea and the United States agreed to a face-to-face meeting, and the United States clearly had the upper hand. Today, the world is closer to a denuclearized North Korea than it has ever been in the past.

NATO PAYS UP

If you've been following along closely, you might have noticed that over the course of the events we've described in this chapter—which don't even scratch the surface of what he's accomplished since being in office—President Trump has managed to fix four out of the five foreign policy problems he pointed out during the campaign, leaving only one to go.

Coincidentally, the problem starts right where this chapter began: under the sixty-foot ceiling of the Andrew W. Mellon Auditorium in Washington, DC. In that building, four years after the end of World War II, President Harry Truman —the man who'd threatened Japan with "a rain of ruin from the air" just a few years earlier—hosted the other Allied nations to sign the North Atlantic Treaty, which established the North Atlantic Treaty Organization (NATO). According to the treaty, each country agreed to spend a certain percentage of its GDP on defense. At the time, the economies of Europe had been destroyed by World War II, so the United States, which accounted for about half of all global output, agreed to pick up most of the slack. At the time, it was the right thing to do, and over the first years, it worked pretty well. But soon, as the economies of the rest of the world recovered, the playing field became even. By the time Donald Trump ran for president, the United States accounted for less than a quarter of all global output, but it was still paying more than the next eight member nations combined for the defense of all NATO member nations.

In short, the United States had stopped acting in its own interest. Instead, we ended up solving everyone else's problems all over the world even though other countries could afford to pay for it themselves. The United States was providing huge benefits to other countries and getting very little in return. During his presidency, Barack Obama had asked—always very politely—whether our allies could maybe, if they felt like it, pay more of their fair share for the services we provided. At the time, only six countries of the twenty-nine in NATO had reached the goal of spending 2 percent or more of their GDP on defense. Altogether, the European countries in NATO spent about $250 billion for their own defense, while the United States spent about $700 billion.

For years, President Trump had seen that this was a massive problem. He had talked about it in the open letter to the *New York Times* that we quoted in the previous chapter, and he'd brought it up in nearly every major policy speech he'd given as a candidate. When he finally won the presidency and started attending meetings with other world leaders, most of them didn't want to go along with his demands. The same pundits who said he was unfit for office in the first place started writing articles about how we were, in fact, getting a fair deal at NATO.

In December 2019, just before the NATO allies gathered in London to mark the seventieth anniversary of the organization, NATO secretary general Jens Stoltenberg announced that going forward, the United States would pay less while other allies would pay more—i.e., exactly what President Trump wanted. "The U.S. will pay less," he said. "Germany will pay more. So now the U.S. and Germany will pay the same, roughly 16 percent of NATO's budget."

Because of Trump's insistence, European countries and Canada are now contributing $130 billion more to NATO than they did in 2016. As President Trump keeps putting pressure on them, that number is sure to increase.

★

Brett Kavanaugh should start suing people for libel, or the Justice Department should come to his rescue. The lies being told about him are unbelievable. False Accusations without recrimination. When does it stop? They are trying to influence his opinions. Can't let that happen!
—@realDonaldTrump, September 15, 2019

★

CHAPTER 10

RIGHT AND JUST

At the beginning of May 2020, as the country was beginning to realize that maybe—just *maybe*—a total lockdown of the country had been a slight overreaction to the coronavirus, members of the United States Senate flew back into Washington, DC, to resume their business. It had been five weeks since they had broken up for an extended recess, and there was a whole pile of work to be done. Aside from showing the country that Congress was ready to open up again, the Senate had to confirm John Ratcliffe, the man President Trump had nominated to be the director of national intelligence. They also had to vote on several Covid-19 relief efforts and pass a big stack of bills pertaining to budgets and other routine congressional matters.

But the biggest story of the day was one that most people weren't even talking about: on Wednesday, May 6, the Senate would vote to confirm a thirty-seven-year-old judge named Justin Walker, the man President Trump had put forward as his nominee for a soon-to-be-vacant seat on the District of Columbia Court of Appeals.

As usual, Democrats weren't happy. On the way in, several of them complained to reporters about having to come back to Washington just to confirm a judge. Senator Chris Coons, a Democrat from Delaware who was notably upset at the fact he had to come in to work, commented condescendingly that "this is not an emergency." Senator Chuck Schumer also did a fair amount of whining, saying "If we *have* to be here, we should at least focus on coronavirus relief." Senator Richard Blumenthal said it was "indefensible" that senators had to come back to town just to confirm a judge who "would dismantle the health care law that is saving millions of lives." Apparently, those people didn't think it was necessary for the Senate to continue conducting business as usual or for the country to begin getting back onto its feet after the virus. They would rather have seen the whole country shut down until election day so that sleepy Joe Biden could win the mail-in vote by a landslide. The left is putting its hopes in ballot harvesting in an attempt to alter the outcome of November's elections.

If you think about it, it makes sense. For the past three years, President Trump has been making the Democrats look like complete morons, at least when it came to getting judges confirmed. Despite their unprecedented obstruction, the president has attained the kind of legislative record that would have seemed impossible just a few years before. He's sent the economy soaring, ended wars in the Middle East, and drastically improved the lives of the working-class Americans who voted for him. Every time he's kept one of his campaign promises—which, as you've probably noticed, is something he did virtually every day—his chances of winning a second term increase exponentially. The Democrats in Congress have tried to stop him at every turn, and at every turn, they have failed.

So the only option they had left was milking the pandemic for as long as they possibly could. As long as the government was shut down, President Trump couldn't get any work done and they would have something to complain about. They knew that every day Congress remained in session, even if it *was* in a mostly empty room with lawmakers calling in via videoconference, some of President Trump's policies would be passed. The more of President Trump's policies that were passed, the better his chances of being reelected would be.

Mitch McConnell was right when he said that if grocery store workers and nurses had to show up to work, senators and congressmen did, too. When he gave the order to have all senators report back to Washington, all those people heard was the sound of levers being pulled for President Trump on election day.

So, yeah. We can see why they didn't want to show up to work.

"LEAVE NO VACANCY BEHIND"

By now you're probably aware of the big promises that President Trump has kept since he took the oath of office. You've been reading about them throughout the entire book. He's made enormous progress on the southern border wall and made Mexico pay for our border security. He's renegotiated our bad trade deals and gotten tough on China. He's made our allies in NATO pay their fair share. But those are the things everyone knows about. Even the liberal media occasionally give him credit for getting them done, as CNN's own

Chris Cillizza did, begrudgingly, in an article on May 18 titled "How Donald Trump Wins Again, in 3 Sentences."

What the Democrats in the Senate were really scared of back in the beginning of May was much, *much* bigger than any of that.

Senators such as Chris Coons and Chuck Schumer, both staunch opponents of the president, know better than anyone that for the past three years, President Trump has been working on another project behind the scenes—one that will have lasting effects on the United States long after he's left office. He's been working on it day and night during his whole first term. In fact, this was the *only* thing everyone with even a tangential affiliation with the GOP agreed on as a priority in the era of Trump's Washington. Since the day he was inaugurated, President Trump has worked closely with Mitch McConnell and Lindsey Graham to completely remake the federal judiciary. And when we say completely, we mean *completely.*

From his first day in office, he has nominated smart, conservative judges to the federal bench at an astonishing rate. Whenever a vacancy on a federal court opens up, he nominates a judge and Mitch McConnell has the Senate confirm them right away. They've become so efficient at pulling off this routine that the *New York Times* referred to the Senate under Mitch McConnell as "a machine for confirming Trump judges." During a speech on the Senate floor in 2017, Senator McConnell famously promised to "leave no vacancy behind," saying that he would fill any and all open seats on the major courts of this country.

Working with the Senate, President Trump has been able to confirm over 200 judges to the federal bench. He has nominated two Supreme Court justices, one of whom sailed right through the confirmation process, the other of whom—well, we'll get to that. He has appointed more circuit court judges by this point in his presidency than any president other than maybe George Washington, and he has plenty more lined up for the rest of 2020. Even without them, though, the numbers are staggering. As of this writing, he has successfully appointed 143 district court judges and 53 judges to the federal courts of appeals.

For perspective, consider the fact that during his eight years in the White House, President Obama nominated only 55 federal judges to those courts in total. By the end of his first term, where President Trump is as of this writing, Obama had nominated only 30. George W. Bush had nominated only 34 at a similar point in his presidency, and Clinton had nominated only 30.

Obviously, this is important. But not everyone realizes *how* important. First of all, federal judges serve lifetime appointments, and a large percentage of the judges President Trump has nominated are under the age of fifty. That means they'll be on the bench for possibly another three decades, ensuring that conservatives will be handing down decisions from the bench for years to come.

For the most part, President Trump has focused his efforts on the appeals courts of the United States. There are thirteen of these courts in the nation, and they're immensely important. Above them, there is nowhere to go but the Supreme Court, which is often called "the court of last resort." However, because only a hundred or so cases a year ever actually get to the Supreme Court, the appeals courts usually get the last word on critical legal issues. When a law is unclear or people get into a disagreement about how to interpret a piece of legislation, they don't go back to Congress for clarification;

the federal courts are where they wage war about what the laws actually mean.

Speaking at Duke University Law School in 2005, future Supreme Court associate justice Sonia Sotomayor, who was nominated by President Barack Obama, admitted that "the court of appeals is where policy is made." Knowing that she shouldn't have said it, she followed up with "And I know this is on tape and I should never say that because we don't make law. I know. Okay, I know. I'm not promoting it. I'm not advocating it. I know."

Everyone "knows." That's why President Trump has been working so hard to make sure those courts are filled with smart constitutional conservatives.

In fact, when we went into the Oval Office to interview President Trump for our second book, *Trump's Enemies*, in September 2018, he was right in the middle of getting a few federal judges confirmed, and he wanted to talk about it. As you can see, even with the Mueller investigation hanging over his head, he was hard at work.

"I've been nominating judges," he said. "You know the only president who nominated more judges than me? George Washington."

After a second, we got the joke.

When we went back to the Oval Office on May 18, 2020, the day President Trump would send shock waves through the White House press corps by announcing that he'd been taking hydroxychloroquine as a preventive measure against Covid-19, we entered to find him signing a stack of papers. Each sheet of paper, he said, contained the name of a judge who'd recently been confirmed by the Senate. All President Trump had to do was sign his name and hand the paper to

Derek Lyons, his staff secretary, and those judges would all have lifetime appointments on the federal bench.

"It's amazing," the president said, rotating among three different pens that had been placed on his desk for the occasion. "I keep sending them judges, and they just keep confirming them."

Every time Democrats in the Senate had had to vote on one of those fifty judges, they were reminded of how successful President Trump had been during his first term. They had also been reminded of how drastically he was changing the United States of America for the better.

That was why they were so unhappy about having to come back to Washington "just to confirm a judge."

CONFIRMATION BATTLES

In a sense, Justin Walker, President Trump's fifty-first nominee to the US Court of Appeals, was just one more point on the board for conservatives. He had already shown that he would interpret the Constitution according to the framers' original intent, stand against government overreach, and fight for the working men and women of the United States. Even the left-leaning American Bar Association, which had rated him "not qualified" in the past, had revised that rating to "qualified" when he was appointed to the appeals court.

Of course, there was no doubt that he was qualified. That's why President Trump nominated him in the first place. In terms of credentials, the man was a slam dunk. Walker had grown up in a small town in Kentucky, where he'd worked for a few years after college in the Senate office of Mitch McConnell himself. He's the only son of a single mother. Time and time again, he had proven that he was a principled conservative who understood the Constitution and was willing to uphold it. He'd gone to Harvard Law School and joined the Federalist Society, a group of conservative lawyers and judges who stand up for traditional American values.

After Harvard, he had clerked for Brett Kavanaugh, who was then a judge on the DC Court of Appeals, and later for Supreme Court justice Anthony Kennedy. Despite his lack of trial experience, which Democrats would screech about for months during the confirmation hearings, he was everything you'd want on the DC Court of Appeals.

He's also outspoken and courageous, which we appreciate. During the contentious confirmation hearing of Brett Kavanaugh, he was on television every week speaking up for his former boss, raising the objections that some other conservatives at the time were too afraid to talk about. He referred to Justice Kavanaugh as a soldier coming out of battle with his uniform "torn and tattered." Speaking at a ceremony held shortly after his nomination, he said this:

> Thank you for serving as an enduring reminder that although my legal principles are prevalent, they have not yet prevailed, and although we are winning, we have not won. And that although we celebrate today, we cannot take for granted tomorrow, or we will lose our courts and our country to critics who call us terrifying and who describe us as deplorable.

That is the kind of judge you get when President Trump is in the White House—not the wishy-washy, go-along-to-get-along kind of guys. You get fighters who are willing to stand up for the conservative principles of ordinary Americans.

No wonder Democrats were worried.

In terms of impact, the DC Circuit Court is a big deal. Often known as the stepping-stone to the Supreme Court, it is where many issues involving the federal government are decided. It's the court that first heard the challenge to the Affordable Care Act, also known as Obamacare, in 2014. Many future Supreme Court justices, from Ruth Bader Ginsburg and Antonin Scalia to Clarence Thomas, John Roberts, and Brett Kavanaugh, served on that court first.

Democrats knew the kind of influence that Walker would have if he ever made it onto the DC Circuit Court, so they went at him with guns blazing. At Judge Walker's Senate confirmation hearing on May 6, 2020, Senator Dick Durbin of Illinois, who was upset that he even had to *be* there, tried to paint Judge Walker as some kind of radical who was going to steal everyone's health care: "You have not been the least bit impartial when it comes to the Affordable Care Act. Your legal or, slash, constitutional contempt is obvious. At your own ceremonial investiture, with a Supreme Court justice standing by you, you mocked it." In terms of attacks, that was about as bad as it ever gets. The judge's record was simply too good to argue with.

As you can see, nothing—not even a once-in-a-century global pandemic—can stop President Trump from keeping his promises. By the end of his second term, he will have had made his mark on the American judiciary unlike any other president ever has before. It doesn't matter what Democrats try to throw at him.

THE BEGINNING

It might be hard to believe now, but confirming judges was not always such a tense political activity. For most of our nation's history, when a judge was nominated, he or she was confirmed shortly thereafter. That was true for district court judges, circuit court judges, and even associate justices of the Supreme Court. As long as the nominee hadn't killed someone or written an opinion that was outrageous, there wasn't much to worry about.

However, all that changed around the late 1970s, when the country really began coming apart at the seams. It was a time of hyperpolarization in American politics, and the courts weren't immune. In the law schools of the United States, something called Critical Legal Studies was becoming popular. This was a system popular among liberals which held that the law wasn't a fair set of rules and regulations that kept society together. Instead, proponents of this theory argued that the law was racist, sexist, and unfair. They said it was a tool designed to keep the lower classes down and the elites in power. Many of the professors who taught it were Marxists, and they had a big influence on some of their students.

When Barack Obama was studying at Harvard Law School, this school of thought was popular. Students and professors believed that once they were on the bench, judges could interpret the law according to "realistic" standards. They believed that the Constitution was a "living document" that could be interpreted according to what society needed at a particular time. So when a ruling about the Second Amendment came before the court, a judge could decide that the Founders couldn't *really* have meant that people were entitled to bear arms—even though that's what they had written— and could rule against it. When a judge heard a case about abortion—as they did during the famous *Roe v. Wade* case of 1973—they could invent a right to abortion, even though there was nothing of the sort in the Constitution. That sideways way of thinking became very popular in the country during the late 1980s and early '90s; even some justices of the Supreme Court, such as Ruth Bader Ginsburg and Stephen Breyer, made their rulings according to it.

In response, conservative thinkers and lawyers all around the country formed a kind of resistance. They believed that the Constitution was not a "living document" or a set of guidelines. They believed, in the words of Justice Antonin Scalia, that the Constitution was "not living but dead, or as I prefer to call it, enduring. It means today not what current society, much less the court, thinks it ought to mean, but what it meant when it was adopted." In that respect, they were in complete opposition to most of their professors, who, especially in the Ivy Leagues, were almost exclusively liberal. In fact, on the day after Ronald Reagan defeated Jimmy Carter for the presidency in 1980, a professor of torts at Yale Law School canceled classes so his students could talk about their feelings and "what was going on in the country." Thirty-six years later, it was even worse: left-wing professors across the country canceled classes after Trump's victory.

In 1982, according to an account of the group's founding by Jeffrey Toobin at *The New Yorker*, Steven Calabresi, a student who'd been in that class at Harvard, decided to form a conservative law society with two of his friends—something to combat the radical leftist agenda that was endemic in law schools all over the country. They decided to call it "The Federalist Society," after a group of American patriots who'd fought for the ratification of the Constitution in 1787. At the University of Chicago Law School, where one of the first chapters of the Federalist Society was formed, the faculty advisor was a young law professor named Antonin Scalia. Back at Yale, where the whole thing had begun, the faculty advisor was a professor named Robert Bork, one of the few men in modern history ever to be denied a seat on the Supreme Court, after he'd been nominated, solely because of his conservativism.

The Federalist Society held its first national conference in 1982 on the campus of Yale University. Antonin Scalia and Robert Bork were both featured speakers, in addition to Ted Olson, who'd become one of the best Supreme Court litigators in the nation. The next year, there were Federalist Society chapters in a dozen law schools. By the early 1990s, there were more than fifty chapters all over the country, and many alumni had been hired to key posts all over the federal government.

One of them was Don McGahn, a young lawyer who'd come right out of law school at Widener University in Chester, Pennsylvania, worked on campaign finance law for a few years in Washington, DC, and then become chief counsel for the National Republican Congressional Committee. Just over a decade later, President George W. Bush nominated McGahn to serve on the Federal Election Commission (FEC), where he went on to become chairman and turned the regulatory machine on its head.

Upon his departure as chairman of the FEC, Citizens United hired Don to sue New York State attorney general Eric Schneiderman for the state's vast overreach in violating Americans' First Amendment rights.

So when Donald Trump called Dave in 2015 and asked for the best campaign finance attorney to work on his still unannounced campaign, he knew exactly who to recommend. First, McGahn had done amazing work at the FEC. Also, Dave knew that most people, himself included, still weren't sure whether to take Donald Trump seriously as a candidate for president. Some assumed he was just doing the whole thing as a publicity stunt and that he would never actually announce. Dave knew that bringing in someone like McGahn, who was a well-respected DC insider, would go a long way toward changing that impression. During the interview between McGahn and Trump, Corey told Mr. Trump Don was the Derek Jeter of campaign finance. Mr. Trump hired him on the spot.

As the campaign wore on and it became clear that Donald Trump was going to win the whole thing, we relied on McGahn's advice even more. When it was time for the campaign to pull together the first list of potential Supreme Court justices, it was Don and Corey who worked to compile the list. When the race was getting very tight and it was time to pull together a second list of names, Don McGahn, Dave, and other team members worked on that project. Having been a lawyer in DC for decades, McGahn knew how important judicial appointments—to the Supreme Court, the circuit courts, and the district courts—could be to a new administration. He helped us seek out the best advice for nominating smart, conservative judges.

As it turned out, McGahn had a close working relationship with Leonard Leo, the president of the Federalist Society. Over the course of its existence, the Federalist Society had made nominating conservative judges to key federal positions one of the core tenets of its mission. When we called on Leo to recommend the best potential nominees to the Supreme Court, he was ready with a long list of names.

When Antonin Scalia died suddenly in 2016, we asked the Federalist Society to help us come up with a few people

Donald Trump could back as possible replacements. We knew that even though Barack Obama would have a shot at naming his own nominee to the bench, Mitch McConnell would do everything in his power to keep the nominee off the floor of the Senate until after the election. So Mr. Leo and the Federalist Society got right to work. Before long, we had a list of twenty-one potential replacements for Scalia, all of whom were tremendously well qualified. When President Trump laid out his famous "Contract with the American Voter" in Gettysburg, Pennsylvania, he made explicit reference to the list. We even printed a PDF of the promises he made during that speech. Finding a replacement for Scalia was one of the most important items on it.

In terms of politics, Antonin Scalia was the last of a dying breed, especially in the world of the Supreme Court. He was an old-fashioned jurist who believed in following the original intent of the Constitution, not interpreting it to mean whatever a judge felt it should mean. If we had allowed him to be replaced with another liberal justice such as Elena Kagan and Sonia Sotomayor, the two justices Barack Obama had nominated to the court, it would have changed the political alignment of this country for decades, tilting the court in a liberal direction permanently.

One of the names on the list from the Federalist Society was Neil Gorsuch, a terrific judge who sailed right through his confirmation process. Despite a few weak attempts by Democrats to dig up old opinions he'd written and decisions they disagreed with, Gorsuch was confirmed as an associate justice of the Supreme Court in 2017. That was an important step in the history of the Supreme Court, and it put us miles ahead of where we might have been if President Obama's choice, Merrick Garland, had been confirmed by the Senate.

But it was nothing compared to what was coming.

On July 9, 2018, Justice Anthony Kennedy announced he was retiring. He had been wanting to get off the court for a while, and he figured he would take the opportunity to do so while there was a Republican president in office. So President Trump consulted with McGahn and his legal team and decided he would nominate Brett Kavanaugh, a brilliant young judge from the District of Columbia Court of Appeals, to succeed Kennedy.

Almost as soon as the name was announced, the knives came out. The usual challenges to Kavanaugh's record started appearing in liberal magazines, of course, as did the ratings by organizations such as the ACLU. But the real trouble began when a woman named Christine Blasey Ford, who'd gone to high school during the same time period as Kavanaugh in the 1980s, accused him of sexual assault. As the confirmation battle wore on, we would come to realize that she remembered close to nothing about the incident she was talking about. She didn't know where it happened, how she got there, or who drove her home. She didn't have any contemporaneous corroborating evidence.

But that didn't stop the media from pouncing on the story. During the month of September, when Kavanaugh was fighting for his life during one of the most turbulent confirmation hearings in recent memory, there were ten stories a day looking not only to corroborate Christine Blasey Ford's story but also to find other women who'd say they'd also been sexually assaulted by Kavanaugh. In *The New Yorker*, a reporter published a piece calling for Kavanaugh to withdraw his name from consideration whether the charges were true or not. In the *New York Times*, the paper's editorial board accused Kavanaugh of "fury and the rawest partisanship" for trying to defend himself against the baseless attacks.

Although Kavanaugh was eventually confirmed, the attacks never stopped. During the month of November 2018—a full two months *after* Kavanaugh had been confirmed—CNN mentioned the Blasey Ford story 1,898 times, MSNBC mentioned it 1,878 times, and Fox News 1,066 times. Two years later, long after Kavanaugh had already heard his first cases, the *New York Times* published an essay from a forthcoming book by two journalists who claimed they had a story from someone who went to school with Brett Kavanaugh at Yale and said that he had "drunkenly thrust his penis into her face." A few weeks later, we learned that the two journalists had never actually talked to the woman and that they'd made the whole thing up based on a rumor. The paper had to issue a correction, but not before it had posted a tweet promoting the story that read in part, "Having a penis thrust in your face at a drunken dorm party may seem like harmless fun."

Yikes.

On the bench, Brett Kavanaugh has conducted himself like a model justice. You'd never know he had to endure one of the most brutal partisan fights in the history of this country to get there. Still, the liberal establishment persists. On his Wikipedia page, the allegations against him take up a full two paragraphs right in the first section. The liberal media can't mention his name without making reference to the fact that they don't think he should be on the bench in the first place. Whenever he issues an opinion or hears a case, there are sure to be five or six articles the next day reminding people of his confirmation hearing. And in case you think these are just people who care about "believing all women" or holding powerful men to account, wait until you read about what happened when a credible, allegedly abused woman accused a certain former vice president of something much worse. You'll be shocked.

So, after watching the Kavanaugh hearings in real time, some of you might be wondering: Why did he go through with them? Was it really that important for him to get onto the Supreme Court, even though he knew the kind of attacks he'd have to endure?

Well, yeah. It was.

A DELICATE BALANCE

On the Supreme Court, one vote—meaning the opinion of one justice out of nine—can mean the difference between winning and losing a case. In fact, as the Supreme Court has become more polarized like the rest of the country, an average of about 20 percent of all cases it hears during a given year are decided by one swing vote, with four justices on the left, four on the right, and one moderate stuck in the middle.

When Donald Trump first announced he was running for president, there were four reliably liberal justices on the court—Ruth Bader Ginsburg, Sonia Sotomayor, Elena Kagan, and Stephen Breyer—and four conservatives—Chief Justice John Roberts, Clarence Thomas, Antonin Scalia, and Samuel Alito—with Anthony Kennedy usually sitting a little right of center. It was a delicate balance that hadn't really gone one way or the other since the 1980s. When one of the justices died or retired, they were usually replaced by someone with the same set of beliefs, so the composition of the court didn't change much.

Still, it made for some nail-biting decisions, which Dave knows better than anyone.

———————————

In 2008, long before Dave had ever met Donald Trump, he was the president of Citizens United, a conservative public policy advocacy organization. Back in 2004, he had seen Michael Moore's *Fahrenheit 9/11* and realized the power of documentary film. *Fahrenheit 9/11* is, to this day, the number one–grossing documentary of all time. Michael Moore brilliantly married politics and documentary filmmaking. It was not just the film's power but its television advertising that dramatically changed American culture that year. There was a point of view and a message that he made entertaining.

By 2007, Citizens United had turned out about half a dozen political documentaries, some of which enjoyed modest success. In 2006, Dave first worked with Stephen K. Bannon on a film titled *Border War: The Battle over Illegal Immigration*. But nothing prepared him for the commotion caused by *Hillary: The Movie*, which began production in 2006 to come out during the 2008 election cycle. The movie, like *Fahrenheit 9/11*, was a mix of documentary and polemic; it had a clear point of view but didn't rely on the old tropes of campaign commercials to make the point. It was entertaining, and people wanted to see it.

However, provisions of the landmark Bipartisan Campaign Reform Act of 2002, commonly referred to as the

McCain-Feingold Act, prohibited Citizens United from broadcasting either the film or ads promoting it. According to the law, it was illegal for a group like Citizens United to show any kind of "electioneering communication" within thirty days of a presidential primary or within sixty days of a general election. The law defined "electioneering communication" as a communication that refers to a clearly identified candidate that is broadcast during the blackout period prior to an election, which—maybe—was what *Hillary: The Movie* was. But then again, it was also more than that.

Following Dave's strategic plan, he had his chief counsel, Michael Boos, work with First Amendment lawyer James Bopp to come up with a solution. One thought was to ask the FEC for an advisory opinion as to whether or not they could show the movie and its advertising on television. Four years earlier, the FEC had ruled that an earlier Citizens United film was not exempt from the ban because Citizens United did not have a sufficient filmmaking track record to qualify as a media company that would be exempt from the ban. However, in late 2017, the FEC lacked a quorum—meaning there weren't enough commissioners to issue advisory opinions—so it couldn't make a ruling on such a request. The only real option was to file a lawsuit in US District Court, which was what Citizens United did. Unfortunately, the three-judge district court panel said its hands were tied by the Supreme Court's earlier ruling upholding the electioneering communications ban for groups such as Citizens United.

There was nothing else to do but appeal to the Supreme Court.

So Citizens United appealed and waited. Finally Dave learned that the Supreme Court would hear the case *Citizens*

United v. FEC, as the case would come to be known. The court had very little choice about whether to take the case because it had jurisdiction over the matter. After the case was granted certiorari, Dave engaged Ted Olson, one of the founding members of the Federalist Society, a former solicitor general of the United States, and the man whom some people have called the tenth justice of the Supreme Court, to represent Citizens United.

When they arrived at the Supreme Court, Dave was stunned. Though he had worked in Washington his whole life, he had never set foot inside the building where the most momentous decisions of the past century had been debated and handed down. The grand hallways, the beautiful marble columns behind the long desk inside the Supreme Court chamber—it was like something out of a movie. When the case began, it seemed as though the whole thing would play out simply. Ted Olson argued that although the FEC rules about "electioneering communications" were fair, they shouldn't apply to documentary films such as *Hillary: The Movie*. Simple as that.

But when Deputy Solicitor General Malcom Stewart got up to argue the government's case, things got interesting. Stewart argued that McCain-Feingold should apply not only to *Hillary* but to all media. He argued, in effect, that a handful of government bureaucrats had the right to tell US citizens what they could and could not publish. It amounted to government censorship, and the justices knew it. A few minutes into the deputy solicitor general's argument, the justices pounced, asking whether the FEC could also use the rules to pull a book off the shelves, even if that book were five hundred pages long and only mentioned the name of a candidate one time in the very last line.

According to federal statute, the solicitor general said, yes, the US government had the statutory power to ban books.

Admittedly, Dave wasn't sure whether they would win or not, but after the oral arguments ended, he had a good feeling. It certainly seemed as though the justices had been on his side. After hearing oral arguments, the justices disappeared to decide his fate. Finally, on the last day of the Supreme Court session, at the end of June, the court shocked the world when Chief Justice Roberts read this message instead of announcing a decision:

> For the proper disposition of this case, should the Court overrule either or both *Austin* v. *Michigan Chamber of Commerce*, 494 U.S. 652 (1990), and the part of *McConnell* v. *Federal Election Comm'n*, 540 U.S. 93 (2003), which addresses the facial validity of Section 203 of the Bipartisan Campaign Reform Act of 2002, Section 441(b) in Title 2 of the United States Code?

When Dave asked Ted Olson what that meant in English, Olson revealed his surprise. "I've only seen this once or twice before," he said. "They want us to come back and argue the case again during a special session of the Supreme Court at the end of the summer."

In the time between the two hearings, Dave got hundreds of phone calls. In a matter of hours, the Citizens United case had gone from dealing with a relatively obscure piece of election law to the First Amendment itself. Even the notoriously liberal ACLU was on his side. In July, Dave got a call from Senate majority leader Mitch McConnell, who expressed an interest in joining his case to defend the right of all Americans to exercise free speech. The Supreme Court approved Senator McConnell joining the case. Dave's team, led by Ted Olson and Matthew McGill in conjunction with Senator McConnell, added the highly respected Floyd Abrams to the team.

In a historic show of just how important the case was, the court reconvened for a special session on September 9, 2009. Special sessions have occurred only on the rarest of occasions, including to determine the outcome of the Bush-versus-Gore election and during the Watergate hearings. On the day Dave and his team went back into the Supreme Court in September, the house was packed. Mitch McConnell also wasn't the only senator who'd walked over from the Senate to watch the proceedings. Across the aisle, just a few feet away, Dave observed senators John McCain of Arizona and Russ Feingold of Wisconsin sitting together. In 1989, Senator McCain had been one of the "Keating Five," a group of politicians who'd been tied to a corrupt businessman from Arizona named Charles Keating. To make up for the embarrassment of that ordeal, he had made campaign finance reform one of his pet projects, working with Senator Feingold to pass legislation that would eventually be known as the McCain-Feingold Act, which put into place many of the FEC restrictions that Dave was fighting against. Sitting in the court that day, they looked nervous.

Because of the importance of the special session, the government leaned on the new solicitor general. This time, a lawyer and former Harvard Law School dean named Elena Kagan, who would later be nominated to the Supreme Court by Obama, was the one arguing the government's case. She knew that the last guy had made a big mess of the government's argument, and she got to work walking it back right away, trying to undo his position on government censorship. She argued that the government didn't *want* to censor the right of people to speak freely, and although it *could* do that, it probably *wouldn't* if—

That was when Chief Justice Roberts interrupted her. Leaning over the bench, he said, as he looked the solicitor general straight in the eye and raised his voice slightly, "But we don't put our—we don't put our First Amendment rights in the hands of FEC bureaucrats."

This wasn't just about election law anymore.

By the end of oral arguments that day, the outcome was clear. Dave looked around as the crowd was leaving the courtroom and found himself standing next to senators McCain and Feingold. He overheard Senator McCain say to Senator Feingold, "Well, Russ, I don't see how we are going to win this thing." It was a moment to savor, and with that statement Dave knew that victory was at hand.

On January 21, 2010, the justices announced their landmark decision. Roberts, Scalia, Kennedy, Thomas, and Alito had voted to reverse the district court's decision and stand with Citizens United, while Stevens, Ginsburg, Breyer, and Sotomayor had voted against. It was a 5–4 decision. In his opinion for the majority, Justice Anthony Kennedy wrote that it could not have ruled otherwise "without chilling political speech, speech that is central to the meaning and purpose of the First Amendment."

If you ever needed proof that one justice can make a difference—that nominating someone to the Supreme Court can have implications that stretch for decades—there it is. If there had been one more liberal judge on the other side, Dave might have ended up losing that case in the Supreme Court. This case helped to level the playing field for conservatives, and is one of the reasons why we worked so hard during the campaign to make sure that President Trump had the best possible people to choose from for the Supreme Court. We wanted to make sure that when it came time for a big decision to be made, whether it was on Obamacare, a travel ban, or the right of Congress to dig through President Trump's finances, there were justices who would uphold the Constitution and rule of law.

LOOKING AHEAD

The fights to confirm Gorsuch and Kavanaugh were important. But in the end, those two justices didn't really tip the balance of the court. Gorsuch replaced Scalia, who was one of the most conservative justices ever to sit on the bench, and Kavanaugh replaced eighty-two-year-old Anthony Kennedy, which moved that seat slightly to the right.

Today, though, the situation is much different. There is a four-four split on the court with the chief justice tending to align with conservatives on some issues. Neither eighty-two-year-old Stephen Breyer, one of the court's most dependable left-leaning justices, or eighty-seven-year-old Ruth Bader Ginsburg, who's been the most extreme liberal on the court for years, will probably serve on the court another full presidential term. A second Trump term would mean altering the Supreme Court for generations to come. Likewise, a Joe Biden term would mean the same thing—but with an entirely different outcome.

That's how important the 2020 election is.

CHAPTER ELEVEN

THE WALL

I am very proud to have brought the subject of illegal immigration back into the discussion. Such a big problem for our country-I will solve
> —@realDonaldTrump, August 26, 2016

At the beginning of January 2020, a caravan of migrants from Central America approached the southern border of Mexico. Months earlier, it had departed from a few small villages in Honduras, and it had been picking up speed over its long journey toward the United States.

Every time this caravan passed through a village or a city along the way, they added more migrants to the group. By the time they arrived at the green gate that separated Mexico from Guatemala, there were about two thousand of them, most of whom were men between the ages of eighteen and thirty. Despite what the liberal media would have you believe, it's not always young, innocent women and children who are trying to slip through the border into the United States. More often than not, it's young men who are hoping to put down roots, get jobs illegally, and then bring their entire extended families over. Sometimes, as President Trump pointed out during his announcement speech, these people bring drugs and crime with them, and according to the Department of Homeland Security, about 12 percent of the people who cross the border illegally every year are engaged in some form of sex trafficking.

By the time this caravan reached the border between Guatemala and Mexico, they stretched back a few thousand feet over the international bridge between Ciudad Tecún Umán, the northernmost town in Guatemala, and the Mexican border town of Ciudad Hidalgo. On the Mexican side, about five hundred soldiers from the Mexican National Guard, all of whom had been dispatched a few days earlier by Mexican president Andrés Manuel López Obrador, stood waiting for them. When the migrants at the front of the pack reached the gates of the bridge, many of them grabbed the bars and started shaking them back and forth. Some tried to climb over the gate. Others stood at a distance, throwing rocks and broken bottles at the soldiers on the other side.

A few minutes later, the soldiers threw tear gas to try to break up the crowd. Many of the migrants jumped off the bridge and into the water, hoping to swim a few hundred feet down the border and cross at a less secure point. But the Mexican National Guard was able to contain the crowd, fighting with it over the next few days to split it up, calm the migrants down, and process their applications for asylum in the proper manner. While there were a few minor flare-ups of violence, the whole thing proceeded peacefully for the most part. In some cases, these people were offered jobs and housing right there in southern Mexico on one condition—they wouldn't be allowed to continue their journey northward toward the United States.

By the end of the day, just over one thousand of those migrants had become Mexican citizens—and not a single one was able to make an illegal entry at the United States border.

The President of Mexico, who acted after speaking with President Trump, had stopped the caravan before it ever reached our border. President Trump's plan had come together.

MEXICO *IS* THE WALL

By now, you probably know that President Trump has no problem getting his message out—especially when that message is about what he's accomplished over the past four years. In terms of reach, he's got the kind of audience that most celebrities would kill for. As of this writing, he has over 82 million followers on Twitter, and he talks right to them every day. When Twitter isn't censoring his thoughts or tagging his tweets with bogus "fact-checks" (which are really just links to their friends in the liberal media), it can be an enormously useful tool. Whenever President Trump has a thought or an idea, you can usually find it on Twitter a few minutes later.

Like it or not, that's just how it is.

As with just about everything else he does, this is calculated. It sends a message to the people that he's not like other politicians, who do their work in secret and then rely on their staffs to present a pretty version of that work to the American public.

Still, he knows how to keep some things under wraps. Since the day he was inaugurated, President Trump has brought a lifetime of lessons from the negotiating table and used them in the Oval Office. One of those lessons involves secrecy. Sometimes it's best to say one thing in public, beating your chest and drawing attention to it, when all the while, you're working on a secret deal under the table.

If you want an example, just look at what he's been able to do with our immigration system. If you believe the reporters assigned to cover President Trump, you would be forgiven for thinking that progress on his "big beautiful wall with a big beautiful door in it" has been pretty slow. In August 2019, for example, the *Washington Post* published a long article checking in on the state of the president's promises. True to form, it twisted the facts to make it seem as though he'd been keeping the public waiting on most of them. But when it got to the wall, saying that it hadn't yet been built and that Mexico wouldn't be paying for it, it was partially correct. Even the conservative *Washington Examiner*, which is usually with the president on the big issues—especially immigration—had to admit that President Trump's administration had not built any new sections of border wall between the U.S. and Mexico, completing only the replacement of dilapidated existing sections.

They had a point. For the first few years of President Trump's first term, House speaker Paul Ryan and his establishment cabal had no interest in passing laws to strengthen the border because it might upset their donors. When the House flipped in 2018, the Democrats formally made stopping the building of the wall their one and only legislative goal. If you gave Nancy Pelosi the choice between solving world hunger or stopping President Trump from finally erecting the wall on the southern border—a project that would have cost just short of $25 billion, by the way, a fraction of what the liberals are asking us to pay for "Medicare for all"—she would stop the wall every time.

There was a good reason for that.

From the moment President Trump came down the golden escalator in Trump Tower, illegal immigration was his signature issue. It was the perfect example of a problem that had been lurking on the fringes of our political discourse for decades, becoming more and more of an emergency every year, but never crept into the mainstream because traditional Republicans were too afraid to bring it up. They all knew that if they raised the issue, they'd be called racist by the left. They knew that if they tried to do something about it, the Democrats would throw up roadblocks every step of the way.

So they danced around the issue. President George H. W. Bush, who'd promised to stem the tide of illegal immigrants who'd been flooding the country since President Lyndon Johnson signed immigration reform into law in the 1960s, did next to nothing about it. Because of his inaction, the rate of people entering the country soared, with apprehensions of illegals going from about 759,000 in 1980 to more than 1.67 million in the year 2000. From there it only got worse.

Much worse, in fact. Officials at the Department of Homeland Security estimated that in the year 2019, after President Trump had been stonewalled by Democrats multiple times on his efforts to get the wall built, about 80,000 people were coming through Mexico and into the United States every month. In May 2019, that number was just under 90,000, the highest it had been since 2007. Because he knew that building the wall would take time—which the American people no longer had—President Trump sought to build his wall in other, more creative ways.

THE ART OF THE DEAL

Early in the summer of 2019, President López Obrador dispatched 20,000 troops to his country's southern border, giving them orders either to turn away the enormous migrant caravans that were coming through his country or to find ways to set them up with jobs and housing in Mexico so they wouldn't reach the border with the United States. Thanks to his policies, the rate of illegal migration to the United States declined significantly. In May 2019, officials at the US Border Patrol apprehended 130,000 migrants at the border. By December of that year, just a few months after the president of Mexico sent troops to *his* southern border, that number was only 32,800. That, for anyone who doesn't know, is a reduction in illegal immigration that this country has *never* seen before. In his book *Defend the Border and Save Lives: Solving Our Most Important Humanitarian and Security Crisis*, former acting ICE director Tom Homan credited President Trump with allowing ICE to finally do its job in a way it had never been able to before.

But did the mainstream media report that? Of course not. They were too concerned with the fact that President Trump, despite repeated promises to build his "big beautiful wall with a big beautiful door in it" on our southern border, hadn't been able to finish the project. For years, they pointed out, he had only been building small sections of the wall and replacing existing structures. One analysis in the *New York Times* noted, with a smug condescension, that out of the 2,000 miles that make up the southern border, President Trump had only been able to build structures on about 122 of them. Another pointed out that Mexico wasn't going to pay for the wall, as

President Trump had promised they would on the campaign trail.

That wasn't the whole story, of course, and we'll explain why in the pages to come. But it didn't matter. Since the day President Trump announced his candidacy and declared that illegal immigration was one of the most serious problems facing this country, the left and the mainstream media had made it their life's work to oppose the wall at all costs.

Nancy Pelosi once declared that the president would "never get his wall under any circumstances." She also said that a wall, in her view, was "an immorality." Senator Chuck Schumer, a Democrat from New York, once made a point of trying to divert all the money that President Trump had set aside to build the wall to gun control initiatives.

The left was so dedicated to destroying the president's agenda that it used every tactic at their disposal, including taking the president to the Supreme Court every time. Pelosi, Schumer, and the Democrat leadership used the courts to stall. From the first proposed travel ban to diverting funding for the wall, they fought the president every inch of the way in order to limit his success.

While Pelosi and Schumer have been screaming about how walls are racist and illegal immigration isn't really a problem, President Trump has been conducting expert negotiations under the table, working with the president of Mexico to ensure that the tide of migrants coming through that country and into the United States would not be allowed to continue. It was a saga unlike anything we'd ever seen play out on the world stage before, and it was conducted largely out of sight of the press and the Democrats. Like a master magician, President Trump has kept the Democrats laser focused on the wall and lesser matters, knowing that as long as they thought they were holding him up, they'd be happy.

Of course, that didn't mean that the people didn't want a wall. One day in July, we saw that for ourselves. We traveled with Donald Trump, Jr., and Kimberly Guilfoyle to the Mexican border to see a few sections of the wall that had been built with private money. The founder of We Build the Wall, Brian Kolfage, explained to us how his organization had been able to do it when no one else could. To this day, it's one of the most incredible things we've seen in American politics. Lots of presidents inspire people to vote, but as far as we know, only President Trump has inspired people to donate money, go to the border, and take up their tools to build the wall.

Projects like that are amazing, and we love seeing Americans working toward a common goal. But to really fix the immigration problem would require different solutions. So while Pelosi and the Democrats were working against him at every turn, President Trump used some of the signature tools of his presidency—tariffs, public pressure, and his world-famous Twitter account—to talk the president of Mexico into helping to stem the tide of illegal immigration.

And it worked.

Speaking with the *Wall Street Journal* about the clash between the Mexican National Guard and the caravans, a man named Irineo Mujica was irate. At the time, he was the head of a group called People Without Borders, and he'd made it his life's work to open the borders of countries—including the United States—to unlimited migration from all corners of the world.

Mujica, speaking for the globalist, open-borders wing, said he was "profoundly disappointed" in the president of

Mexico's actions, going on to say that he didn't like any situation that handed President Trump a win. "López Obrador and Mexico," he said, "have become Trump's wall."

Well, clearly, we're pissing off the right people. As you can see, not only has President Trump talked Mexico into paying for the wall, as he promised he would, he has made Mexico into one giant wall without spending one penny of taxpayer money. However, we're not taking any chances and we are still building our own big beautiful wall.

The story of how he did it and how Democrats failed to stop him despite focusing 110 percent of their energy on the task is a master class in modern leadership. President Trump was willing to put his reputation on the line, change his goals in real time, and compromise with foreign leaders who had initially opposed him, all so he could secure our borders and keep American citizens safe.

When historians write the full history of the Trump presidency in a few decades, the president's progress on the border is sure to be one of the defining episodes—not only of President Trump's first term but of his whole career in politics.

TO THE BORDER

In July 2015, Corey recommended that Donald Trump visit the Mexican border—and made sure he did it the right way. He didn't want to set up a camera, position Mr. Trump so you could just barely make out the border in the background, and then have him give a speech that made it look as though he was really in the danger zone. Mr. Trump wanted to see the places where the crisis of illegal immigration was real for people.

So we went to Laredo, Texas, a city that sits right on the US border with Mexico. The town embraced the Trump visit.

There was a full police detail, a presidential-size motorcade with two buses full of reporters, and dozens of police escorting Mr. Trump through the city and to the border. By doing this, Donald Trump was telling the people of the United States that he wasn't afraid to face the carnage that he might encounter at one of the most dangerous places in the country. In an interview with Fox News conducted on the day before he left, Trump said, "I may never see you again, but we're going to do it."

Just over a year later, after Donald Trump had become his party's nominee for president, he took another trip to the Mexican border—but this time it was planned in secret and precautions were put into place to ensure his safety. At the time, the Mexican president was Enrique Peña Nieto, who had invited both Donald Trump and Hillary Clinton to meet with him about the relationship between the United States and Mexico, especially as it pertained to immigration. Of course, Donald Trump was the only one willing to make the trip. However, Mr. Trump couldn't fly his 757 with his name on it into Mexico. So the campaign made arrangements to borrow his friend Phil Ruffin's unmarked Global Express for the surprise journey. Dave was stunned when he walked into Steve Bannon's office and Steve told him Trump was going to Mexico on a secret trip. It was a brash move by a brash candidate from a brash campaign, and it paid off.

In going to meet with President Peña Nieto, Donald Trump sent another clear message to the American people: he wasn't going to wait around for the election to solve the immigration problem. If other heads of state from around the world invited him to visit, he was going to go. During that trip, he took his first steps toward convincing the world that he could not only be tough on Mexico, forcing it to get control of its immigration problem, he could also negotiate with its leaders. Although President Peña Nieto would be out of office by the time he became president, he would negotiate with Peña Nieto's successor to stop the flow of illegal immigrants coming into the United States. It remains one of his signature policy achievements, and it's something only he could have done.

★

Joe Biden is a reclamation project. Some things
are just not salvageable. China and other countries
that ripped us off for years are begging for him.
He deserted our military, our law enforcement and
our healthcare. Added more debt than all other
Presidents combined. Won't win!

—@realDonaldTrump, July 6, 2019

★

CHAPTER TWELVE

SLEEPY JOE BIDEN

Look, by now it should be pretty obvious that we don't think Sleepy Joe Biden has much of a shot at winning this race; however, with the mainstream media serving as an extension of the Democratic Party, anything is technically possible. Even if you ignore the obvious things, from the credible accusation of sexual assault to the outright lies he's been caught in over the past few decades, the outcome still seems obvious—or at least it docs up here in the daylight, which Biden hasn't seen for a few months now because he's been in his basement.

As of this writing, there are still a few months left in the campaign of 2020, and Biden is in bad shape. If elected, he will be seventy-eight years old when he is sworn in, making him the oldest person ever to assume the presidency. Can you imagine him serving two full terms? He would be eighty-six at the end of his second term. At his advanced age, statistically speaking, it's not likely he would serve out a full term in the White House. From where we're standing, it looks as though a team of advisors choreograph every move and write every word he says to try to limit his gaffes. If you want proof that he's not up to the job, just listen to the guy speak for a few seconds. Chances are that's all the proof you'll need.

Toward the beginning of the campaign, for instance on February 25, former Vice President Biden forgot that he was running for president, asking the people who'd gathered to hear him speak in North Carolina to elect him senator. On February 22, he had said that his son Beau had been the attorney general of the United States, when he'd actually been AG of Delaware. A few weeks after that, he lamented that President Trump wasn't doing enough "economic intercourse" with China—whatever the hell *that* means. And of course, on May 22, Joe famously said during a radio interview that "If you have a problem figuring out whether you're for me or Trump, then you ain't black."

Clearly, something is going on here. We're not doctors, and we didn't stay in a Holiday Inn Express last night, but we think it's fair to speculate by now that Sleepy Joe is not exactly—you know—*all there* anymore.

Then again . . .

What were the chances of a once-in-a-century pandemic sweeping the globe and shutting down the entire country for a solid three months? Probably about 2 or 2.5 percent, right? Clearly, just because something is very unlikely doesn't mean it can't happen. If you'd told us a year ago, for example, that we'd be publishing this book in the middle of a campaign that's being conducted almost entirely on webcams, in basements, and without a single Trump rally in months, we'd have thought you were insane. Also, not that we like making this comparison, but a 2 percent chance of victory is almost exactly what the *New York Times* and the rest of the Fake

News pollsters gave *us* during the 2016 election. Even in the final hours of the evening, when Dave was running with the newly elected President Trump down to the Grand Hyatt hotel in midtown Manhattan and Corey was watching from the set of CNN in Washington, DC, they were treating us with the same arrogant, dismissive attitude that we're currently using to describe Sleepy Joe Biden's campaign.

Again, we don't think it's likely, but as we've learned over the past few months, nothing is guaranteed. Sometimes, as we've all come to find out, shit happens.

SMALL TOWN JOE

If we're going to do this, we might as well go back to the beginning, all the way back to the town of Scranton, Pennsylvania, where Joe Biden was born. If you listen to Biden long enough, you're bound to hear that it was in that small town that he learned his hardscrabble approach to politics. It was where he grew up beside coal miners and owners of small-town businesses. During a famous speech at one of the early-1988 presidential debates—yes, we said 1988—Joe Biden would also refer to this town as the place where his father, a coal miner, used to play catch with him in the yard.

Well, as always, the truth is a little more complicated.

Biden's father was a car salesman, and he moved the family to Delaware when Biden was eleven. Unless Sleepy Joe wandered into a mine shaft by accident sometime during the first eleven years of his life, he has no idea what life is like for coal miners. In fact, there's not a single shred of evidence that anybody in the Biden gene pool was ever a coal miner, although that wouldn't stop Biden from claiming they were over and over again during his first run for the presidency.

From the moment he was elected to the Senate at the age of twenty-nine, Biden made the small-town regular-guy attitude part of his general approach to the world. During his years in the Senate, he would commute back and forth between Washington, DC, and Wilmington, Delaware, on Amtrak, palling around with the conductor and train staff, often posing for photo ops.

Despite his limited national exposure, Biden decided to run for president in 1987, joining a group of six other Democratic candidates who would eventually be dubbed "the Seven Dwarfs" by a newspaper columnist. During that race, as members of his campaign would later report to the *New York Times*, he developed a strange aversion to the truth. He would often keep crowds in their seats for hours at a time, telling long stories about past scrapes with his buddies—that was where some of the themes he'd return to over and over again first appeared—and his noble past in the civil rights movement, which he told many stories about even though he had never marched in the Civil Rights movement.

Over and over again, he treated crowds to that speech. He also got mean with his audiences, accusing someone who'd asked him a question about his "not having a very high IQ." In February 1987, Biden lifted a few lines from a speech that Robert F. Kennedy had once given about the importance of education. At first nobody noticed. But soon an official from the Reagan White House, political director Jeffrey Lord, who'd been an admirer of RFK, wrote a letter to the *New York Times* pointing out the plagiarism. It didn't take long for reporters to start digging through some of Biden's other speeches. Over the course of a few months, they found that Biden had borrowed liberally from Hubert Humphrey, John

F. Kennedy, and a British politician named Neil Kinnock. Turned out that there wasn't too much original about "working-class Joe" at all.

In August 1987, during the first debate during the 1988 race, Biden pulled out this little story, once again recalling his hardscrabble upbringing in the coal-mining towns of Pennsylvania. He asked the crowd why he was "the first in his family ever to go to a university," and why his relatives, who "read poetry and wrote poetry and taught [him] how to sing" never got to go. In the end, he said it was because they didn't have a platform upon which to stand.

A few weeks later, according to an account of the matter that would be printed in the *Washington Post*, a political reporter from Des Moines, Iowa, recorded Biden's speech on videotape. He then compared it to another videotape that had been floating around Washington for a few months. That one showed a British politician named Neil Kinnock, who had produced a commercial for his own campaign back in May of that same year.

The reporter gave the videotapes to Paul Tully, a campaign staffer for Michael Dukakis, and told him to watch them one after the other. When Tully put on the video of Neil Kinnock, he saw another man wondering why he had been the first in his family to go to "university," and why his acestors who could "dream dreams" and "see visions" never got to go." No surprise, he also said it was because they didn't have a platform upon which to stand.

Reading those two speeches side by side, you almost wonder whether Biden really believed he could get away with it. Back then, as we know all too well, it really *was* possible for politicians to tell lies and get away with them (at least compared to today). If a candidate like Bill Clinton had been running in the year 2020, for instance, with all the opportunities for catching a candidate in the act, he would never have been elected governor of Arkansas.

Of course, Joe Biden didn't seem to have much to hide. Immediately following his election to the Senate, his wife and daughter died in a tragic car accident. The sympathy of the nation was with him. He had a youthful energy, and he could speak extemporaneously in ways that were genuinely moving, but when he dropped out of the 1988 race for president, everyone was sure he'd be back.

SWAMPY JOE

After Joe Biden dropped out of the race, he went back to the Senate, where he stayed for the next two decades, taking only the occasional break to contemplate running for president again. During his time in Washington, he got older and became a favorite in the Swamp. No longer the young reformer he once was, he started cutting the kinds of backroom deals you read about in old-fashioned political novels.

The process was simple: he would take a big donation from a major company, then go represent that company's interests in Congress. It's not exactly illegal, according to the rules, but it is a pretty scummy thing that many career politicians do.

During the years Biden was in Congress, he would pull the move over and over again, especially when it came to credit card companies. Over and over again, big credit card companies would give him donations, and in return, he would pass legislation that worked to their benefit. In the early 2000s, he accepted a few major donations from MBNA, one of the biggest credit card companies in Delaware. Years earlier, his son

Hunter—about whom you'll hear *much* more later—got a job on the board of that company, earning exactly $100,000 a year despite having absolutely no experience in the industry. Even when Hunter officially became a lobbyist in 2001, he continued to draw the same salary. (This is a theme that would play out over the course of Hunter's career.)

In 2005, acting at the behest of MBNA, Senator Biden helped pass a bill that made it much harder for Americans to declare bankruptcy. At the time, nearly 2 million Americans were filing for bankruptcy every year, and the credit card companies were losing major profits because of it. Because most of the people didn't make very much money, they were able to declare something called Chapter 7 bankruptcy, which allowed them to sell their assets and then liquidate their debts, rather than Chapter 13 bankruptcy, which required some portion of their future income to go toward creditors. After Senator Biden passed the 2005 Bankruptcy Abuse Prevention and Consumer Protection Act, declaring bankruptcy became nearly impossible—but it didn't fix the underlying problem. Millions of working-class Americans were still in dire financial straits, and Congress wasn't helping them out.

According to Bruce Markell, a professor of bankruptcy law and practice at Northwestern University who spoke to the *Washington Examiner* about the law fifteen years later, it was like "someone looking at a hospital and saying, 'oh my God, emergency admissions are way up.' So the solution is to reduce the hours of the emergency room."

Obviously, it wasn't a bill that anyone who used to call himself "Joe Six-Pack" would have supported. It's also not something that anyone who cares about the American worker would have supported. Experts estimate that some of the provisions in the law—one of which makes it nearly impossible to effectively refinance or cancel student loan debt—is responsible for creating the student debt crisis we're in now. Of course, Biden didn't care. Aside from campaign donations, he was also supported by the credit card companies in other ways. In February 1996, for example, an executive at MBNA bought Joe Biden's home in Delaware for $1.2 million, even though similar houses in the area were going for around $200,000 less than that. The same guy donated thousands of dollars to Biden's Senate reelection campaigns, and in total, his company donated a total of $304,475 to the campaign.

Of course, Biden wasn't acting alone. All that corruption is hard for one guy to handle. So along with his son Hunter, who was already a DC lobbyist making hundreds of thousands of dollars a year trading off his father's name and influence, Senator Biden brought his brother Jim into the fold. For years, Jim had known that he had a massive opportunity in making people "invest in" his brother. From Joe's very first years in the Senate, Jim had been there. In 1973, just one year after Joe was elected to the Senate, Jim got what *Politico* would later classify as "very generous bank loans" to open a nightclub. When the nightclub ran into trouble and was forced to close down, Joe Biden had to step in, telling the *News Journal* "What I'd like to know is how the guy in charge of loans let it get this far."

After his initial adventures in nightclubs and running Joe Biden's Senate campaigns, Jim Biden also became a lobbyist, opening a company in the 1990s that helped lawyers in Mississippi who were involved in litigation for the tobacco industry. For help, he enlisted Hunter Biden, and that's when the real trouble began. At the time, Hunter Biden was still being paid around $100,000 a year by the credit card company MBNA, which had led to Joe Biden being known as "the senator from MBNA." In 1999, he denied it, saying "I am *not* the senator from MBNA." Together, Hunter and Jim launched several investment efforts, always sure to mention that they were related to the senator from Delaware. It was bad enough that in 2005, Joe Biden convinced his son Hunter to leave lobbying work for good to avoid the appearance of impropriety.

What he did instead wasn't much better. Now that he was out of the lobbying game, Hunter had time to join his uncle in investing full-time, and they got busy. In 2006, for example, Jim and Hunter called a meeting at a firm called Paradigm Global Advisors, which they were going to acquire using money they'd made together. At some point during the meeting, according to *Politico*, Jim Biden said, "We've got people all around the world who want to invest in Joe Biden." Then, after being reprimanded for saying it, according to an investigation by *Politico*, he kept going, saying "We've got investors lined up in a line of 747s filled with cash ready to invest in this company."

Eventually, they did acquire the company.

That kind of thing continued for years, all the way up until Joe Biden became the running mate of Barack Obama and eventually the vice president of the United States. Then the corruption *really* started.

FROM CHINA TO UKRAINE

In December 2013, Hunter Biden accompanied his father on Air Force Two (incidentally, Joe Biden refuses to disclose all the trips Hunter took on Air Force Two) on a trip to China, where the vice president would be meeting with Chinese president Xi Jinping. On its face, Hunter was tagging along for the chance to see China with his father, which isn't uncommon in presidential families. However, Hunter also had some business to attend to.

As soon as they got off the plane, Hunter and Joe ended up in the lobby of their hotel talking to a man named Jonathan Li, who had just become a business partner of Hunter's in a private equity firm he'd cofounded in China. According to reports, Hunter thought it might grease the wheels a little if he could arrange a photo op between his new business partner and his father.

During that trip, Hunter Biden and his partners managed to scare up an alleged $1.5 billion for their new fund, even though they had very little experience in investing or knowledge of the markets they were about to get into. It's important to note that in many of the dealings, Hunter Biden was dealing with banks in China, which are effectively arms of the Chinese Communist government. When we talk about Joe Biden not having an incentive to get tough on China the way President Trump has, *this* is the kind of stuff we're talking about.

Of course, that trip to China was just the beginning, as Hunter would set his sights on Ukraine. As we would all come to know because of the Democrats' bogus impeachment investigation against the president, he also served on the board of a corrupt Ukrainian gas company called Burisma Holdings, which paid him over $80,000 per month for his work. If you're trying to figure it out, that's $20,000 a week, or about four grand a day! Once again, Hunter Biden had no relevant experience in the industry, and he certainly didn't speak Ukrainian. In testimony a few years later—after he got caught—Hunter Biden would admit on morning television that he probably wouldn't have gotten the job if his last name wasn't Biden.

At the time Hunter was on the board, Burisma was being investigated for corruption. The prosecutor in charge was a man named Viktor Shokin, who had been looking into the company for a little over a year. Suddenly, once things started getting heated, Joe Biden, who was acting as the Obama administration's point man on Ukraine, began pressuring the government to fire Shokin. Years later he would brag about it on video, saying that he had threatened to withhold $1 billion in critical US aid if the prosecutor wasn't fired. Then, as Biden tells it, "Well, son of a bitch, he got fired." That was how the legend of Quid Pro Quo Joe was born.

When that was reported in the United States, nobody really cared very much. In fact, the only time it ever made headlines in liberal newspapers was when people were mad at President Trump for pointing out that something corrupt had happened. Obviously, when you're a Democrat, you can be corrupt as you like and nobody is going to call you on it. You can serve on the boards of foreign companies, get money improperly, and trade off the name of your well-connected relatives all day long. As long as you're not a Republican, nobody is going to care.

The same, it turns out, goes for sexual assault.

#NOTME

Remember Supreme Court Associate Justice Brett Kavanaugh? The upstanding judge whose entire confirmation process was almost torpedoed because someone who attended high school at the same time said that maybe one time, but I don't really remember when, this guy sexually assaulted me?

The liberal media was all over that one. On two separate occasions, the *New York Times* editorial board called for Kavanaugh's confirmation to be stopped. For days, they refused to dig into the actual details of what Christine Blasey Ford was asserting, instead choosing to take everything she said at face value. They wanted to take down Kavanaugh, and she was the only chance they had.

With Tara Reade, however, it was a different story.

As far back as 1993, when Biden was a senator from Delaware who'd run for president once and failed, Reade had been sounding the alarm bells in her local paper. According to the testimony she gave to the Grass Valley, California, newspaper *The Union*, Biden used to rest his hands on her shoulders for way too long when she was working as an aide in his Senate office. When they had events, he used to ask her to serve drinks because "he liked her legs." She didn't say anything because she wanted to be seen as professional.

Then, as the campaign of 2020 was heating up and Biden—against all odds—actually managed to become his party's nominee, Reade told the world something she'd been holding back: she said that one night, after working late in the office, Biden had forced her up against a wall and forcibly penetrated her with his fingers, whispering into her ear the whole time. Not only had she told her friends immediately after it happened, her then husband alluded to it in court documents around that time. Soon after she made her allegation, it was revealed that a woman who claimed to be her mother had called in to *Larry King Live* in 1993 to say that her daughter had been assaulted by a "very powerful man" in Washington. Clearly, it was a credible allegation, unlike the one lobbed at Brett Kavanaugh. These claims were much more serious, and the accuser had contemporaneous evidence and corroborating witnesses. More troubling were the power dynamics at play: the acts Reade endured were committed when Biden was a sitting senator and her boss.

When you consider Biden's track record on sexual assault allegations, the picture gets much clearer. During the confirmation hearings of Clarence Thomas, for instance, which took place in 1991 when Biden was chairman of the Senate Judiciary Committee, a young woman named Anita Hill accused Thomas of sexual harassment. Keep in mind that Clarence Thomas is a conservative, so for all intents and purposes, Biden had every reason to be on Anita Hill's side in that situation.

But his actions didn't make it seem that way. As the senators on the committee lobbed inappropriate questions at Hill, repeatedly calling her a liar on national television, Biden stood by and did nothing. Over the objections of his left-wing colleagues, he never jumped to her defense. In the end, Biden would vote against Clarence Thomas, but the Senate would confirm Thomas anyway.

Twenty years later, when Tara Reade made her first accusations against Biden, the media didn't bring up Biden's record of ignoring the stories that abused women told. Instead, they got to work discrediting Reade in every way they possibly could. Within a few days, the headlines started coming. The *Washington Post* published a piece called "Trump Allies Highlight New Claims Regarding Allegations Against Biden." At CNN they published a piece called "A Complicated Life and Conflicting Accounts Muddle Efforts to Understand Tara Reade's Allegation Against Joe Biden." Eventually, Reade had a chance to tell her story to Megyn Kelly—on YouTube because no liberal cable news channel would book her—and her account was very compelling. But again, nobody picked it up.

Once again, when it happens to a Democrat, the rules are different. Shortly after the media had made the allegations against Biden go away for good, the *New York Times* published its final word on the subject, headlined "'Believe All Women' Is a Right-Wing Trap." That was just nineteen months after "Believe All Women" became the rallying cry against Kavanaugh's confirmation—so no, it wasn't a "right-wing trap."

By the end of the ordeal, Biden had said very little. He had given a few interviews about the matter, always dismissing it quickly, and said during a campaign event that "I wouldn't vote for me if I believed Tara Reade." He has refused to allow anyone to examine roughly thirty-six years of his Senate records, all of which are secretly held at the University of Delaware.

Obviously, Biden is attempting to hide his Senate record from the American people so he can conceal his conversations with world leaders such as Russian president Vladimir Putin as well as his radical Senate voting record. Further, he wants to conceal his close working relationships with known Democrat segregationists such as Ku Klux Klan Grand Wizard, Senator Robert Byrd of West Virginia; Senator James "The Voice of the White South" Eastland of Mississippi; and Senator Herman Talmadge of Georgia. Everyone is saying those records contain further evidence of inappropriate conduct with Chinese and Russian officials as well. If Dave's experience digging through evidence has taught him anything, most of the documents need to be examined page by page. You can't just run them through a scanner and find out what's on them. At one point, an expert estimated that going through all the data to find Reade's original complaint could take about six months, which, conveniently, was about how long was left until the election.

AN AMERICAN TRAGEDY

Even with the entire liberal media on his side, Joe Biden probably doesn't stand a chance of winning this election. Don't believe us? All you have to do is listen to him speak for a few minutes, and the very notion of his sitting behind the Resolute Desk, dealing with leaders such as China's Xi Jinping, North Korea's Kim Jong-un, and Russia's Vladimir Putin will seem ridiculous.

But again, you never know. Just in case you weren't motivated to get out and vote before, take a minute and imagine what life might be like if the unbelievable does happen and Joe Biden is elected president of the United States this November.

For the past five chapters, we have been outlining the historic accomplishments of President Trump's first four years in office. This is a record that has no precedent in modern American history, and it's not likely to be replicated anytime soon. Clearly, nobody but President Trump could have stood up to brutal dictators like Kim Jong-un on the world stage, reduced taxes for hardworking families, *and* nominate a record number of conservative judges all at the same time.

Those are amazing accomplishments, but they're not permanent.

In fact, other than the federal judges—who have lifetime appointments no matter what the Democrats have to say about it—almost everything that President Trump has done over the last four years is reversible.

If Sleepy Joe Biden gets into office, his first order of business will almost certainly be to dismantle every single one of President Trump's accomplishments. From the beginning, his campaign has been about nothing other than hatred of Donald Trump, and we have no reason to doubt that his administration—if, God forbid, there is one—would be about largely the same thing.

If Biden takes office in January, he'll nominate federal judges. Whether the Senate is controlled by Republicans or Democrats, eventually he will nominate some of the most liberal judges this country has ever seen—not the sensible, measured conservatives whom President Trump has been naming to the federal bench. You can bet that if Sleepy Joe enters the White House, Ruth Bader Ginsburg and Stephen Breyer will take the opportunity to retire, giving his administration the chance to nominate two die-hard liberals to the Supreme Court. After that, it would take only one more to knock the whole court off balance, putting everything from religious freedom to our First, Second, and Fourth Amendment rights at stake.

On the southern border, Biden would stop all progress on President Trump's border wall, letting the sections that have already been built fall into disrepair. During an interview he gave on May 14, 2020, he said that although he wouldn't end construction on the wall, he "wouldn't be spending a lot of money on it." In other words, even though Sleepy Joe knows that illegal immigration to the United States is a massive problem—one that he proposed fixing in 2006 with about 700 miles of fence—he doesn't have the strength to face down the radical wing of his own party and fight for one. So far, President Trump is the only man in modern history who has taken on this fight and won. If Joe Biden wins the White House, our southern border will be wide open, he will give free health care to illegals, the president of Mexico will know that he's no longer dealing with the world's toughest negotiator, and the number of illegal immigrants coming into this country every year will be even higher than during the Obama-Biden years.

On the world stage, Biden would be embarrassing. He would not have the strength—or the ability—to engage in a verbal back-and-forth with Kim Jong-un the way President Trump did. Nuclear powers like North Korea and Iran would get the message that it was okay to begin developing nuclear weapons again because they would know that the man in the White House wouldn't want to waste political capital trying to stop them. After all, it was Joe Biden who helped Barack Obama negotiate the Iran nuclear deal, which ended with our shipping more than $1.74 billion in cash to Iran on pallets. For thugs and dictators abroad, a Biden presidency would be a dream come true.

Of course, what he'd do with our enemies is nothing compared to the damage he could do to our relationships with our allies. At several points during the campaign, he has said that President Trump's fixation on getting members of NATO to contribute more is a waste of time, and he's used photographs of President Trump's confrontational meetings with our allies—meetings that put tens of millions of dollars more into NATO's coffers—to convince American voters that the president is not respected on the world stage. Obviously, that couldn't be further from the truth. Under his presidency, the "America First" doctrine would disappear, replaced by the globalist agenda prevalent during the Obama years, back when we were told that rapid economic growth was impossible and the president would need a magic wand to fix the economy.

During the campaign, Biden also met with several groups that pressured him to cut military spending. If he listened to these groups, which include Demand Progress, Code Pink, Greenpeace, and MoveOn, he would end up cutting the Defense Department's budget by $200 billion every year, and he would also "reverse some of Trump's biggest military priorities, such as refurbishing the U.S. nuclear arsenal and shelving the creation of the Space Force as the sixth branch of the military," according to a report in *Foreign Policy*. Now, those aren't the kinds of policies you want to announce during a campaign. Nobody is going to get excited that you're *not* pursuing the space force or that you're decreasing funding to the people who keep us safe. But make no mistake, this is *exactly* the kind of thing that Democrat administrations have been doing for years: they keep quiet about things during the campaign, and then when they get into the White House, they reveal their real priorities. If Sleepy Joe Biden gets behind the Resolute Desk, our military will be among the first things he cuts.

It's also important to remember that if Joe Biden comes to the White House, he wouldn't be coming alone. You can bet that the whole Obama crew, or at least people who believe in the same things they did, will come right back with him. Beyond the regular establishment Democrats, that means that socialists such as Alexandria Ocasio-Cortez, who's been advising Biden on the environment and the Green New Deal, might actually get a position in the White House. If she does—even if she doesn't—you can bet that the United States would be back in the Paris Agreement faster than you could say "hydrocarbon emissions." That would cost American taxpayers billions of dollars every year and tens of thousands of jobs, and so would the hundreds of regulations that Joe Biden would put back into place if he ever got to the Oval Office.

Of course, the most important issue of the next four years will probably be the US government's efforts to recover from the effects of the Covid-19 pandemic. If we stick with President Trump, he will continue to put our economy back on the road to recovery, helping blue and red states alike to come back from the disaster that the pandemic wrought. He's already shown he can do this during his first term. During his second term he will guide the world's economic rejection of China, a country that unleashed the disease on the world after keeping it secret.

If Joe Biden is president, he will live by the Rahm Emanuel axiom "Never let a crisis go to waste." He'll bow to blue-state governors, including Andrew Cuomo of New York and Gretchen Whitmer of Michigan, all of whom have every intention of sucking every last dollar they can out of the federal government. They have been running their states into the ground for years, and they believe that it's the federal government's responsibility to bail them out—using money from red states—just because there was a pandemic. Joe Biden would allow it to happen; President Trump will not.

And then there's China. After reading about Joe Biden's ties to this country during this chapter, do you really think anyone in the Communist Party will take him seriously when he comes to the negotiating table? Even if the Chinese don't have some kind of compromising information about further deals that Hunter Biden did when he was there—and we don't know whether they do or don't—there is no way that Joe Biden can effectively negotiate with President Xi Jinping or the others who are running the authoritarian regime. Hunter Biden's firm BHR was involved in many other questionable deals together with the Chinese government, including the Henniges Automotive and China molybdenum deals.

Now is the time for Americans to stick with what has worked for us, and what has worked for us in the past—often twenty-four hours a day, nonstop, never taking breaks for meals or sleep—is President Donald J. Trump. Donald Trump didn't run for office for money or fame. No, he did it because he truly cares about the direction of our country and wants to leave it in a better place for our children and grandchildren. Just as he told Oprah in 1988, when the first specter of a Donald Trump run for president hit the mainstream media, "I do get tired of seeing what's happening with this country, and if it got so bad, I would never want to rule it out totally, because I really am tired of seeing what's going on with this country, how we're really making other people live like kings, and we're not."

The heavyweight champion of the world fights nonstop.

It's really not a tough choice, but it is one that will have a lasting impact on the direction of 330 million American lives. Let's hope the American electorate makes the right decision.

CHAPTER THIRTEEN

TRUMP 2020

*I think we're going to have a tremendous rebound.
There's a great energy and a great pent-up demand.*

—President Trump, April 1, 2020

I t used to be that presidential political campaigns were pretty predictable. Every four years, Americans were told that this was the most critical presidential election of our lifetime.

Every four years, we were told that the presidential candidates' policies and beliefs couldn't be further apart.

Every four years, we were promised a bold new direction.

And every four years we got the same old same old. The two candidates were always, in reality, on the same Washington establishment team.

Then came 2016.

Donald Trump, a first-time candidate without a political machine, took on Hillary Clinton, the consummate Washington, DC, insider and the successor to the Clinton Dynasty.

This time, the candidates' visions for America were fundamentally different. Hillary represented a globalist world view; Donald Trump espoused an unapologetic "America First" agenda.

Clinton favored open borders and wanted to continue lousy trade deals; Trump touted a merit-based immigration system, a big, beautiful wall, and the renegotiation of trade deals to finally benefit the United States.

We don't have to tell you what happened.

You'd think after the drubbing the Democrats took in 2016, they would have learned their lesson. Fat chance.

In Joe Biden, they once again chose a globalist.

In Biden, they again chose a candidate who wants illegal immigrants to overrun our social safety nets.

In Sleepy Joe, they once again chose the ultimate Washington Swamp creature.

Donald Trump, after four years in office, is still the outsider.

Based on the body of work from his first term, our personal relationship with the president, and his unwavering desire to put America First, we have a good idea of what his second term would look like.

Before we get to the policies that will enrich the lives of every American, there's one other thing you can bank on in a Trump second term: the president will remain the outsider and continue to do everything he can to disrupt the status quo.

The Swamp, it turned out, was deeper and more entrenched than even the president believed. If Robert Mueller and little Adam Schiff taught us anything, it was that the tentacles of the Deep State reached into all corners of the government.

Whether it's in the bowels of Foggy Bottom, or at the NSC, or inside the West Wing, the president has promised to root out the bad actors until the last of them is out of government for good.

There is an old axiom in Washington that goes, "Personnel is policy." Too often during President Trump's first term, people were put into positions of power who shouldn't have been. People such as Rex Tillerson and John Kelly actively tried to thwart the president's agenda. Not only will the president continue to root out the bad actors, he'll keep the unelected bureaucrats and self-important individuals who don't share his "America First" agenda from getting through the door in the first place.

Changing personnel will allow the administration to be even more successful than it was during its first term. With the right staff in place and a renewed mandate from the American people, it will create new opportunities for even greater success in Donald Trump's second term.

We've gone over what the president has already accomplished, so now let's take a look at what lies ahead—what Americans would get in a second Trump term.

JOBS

At a 2016 town hall meeting in Elkhart, Indiana, a steelworker complained to President Obama about the many jobs that we were losing to Mexico and overseas. Obama told the worker that some jobs "are just not going to come back." His remark was typical of the defeatist attitude that was the hallmark of his presidency. There are plenty of examples of this. Remember his "apology tour"? He traveled to countries on three continents to beg for forgiveness for everything that Americans stand for. Remember, "If you've got a business—you didn't build that." How about the PBS town hall when he told the audience that if Donald Trump was going to negotiate better trade deals, he'd need a magic wand?

When Donald J. Trump took office, he inherited a sluggish economy with low GDP growth, stagnant wages, and entire industries fleeing the United States, taking jobs with them. By never giving up on American jobs, negotiating better trade deals, and putting into effect game-changing tax cuts, President Trump has built the greatest economy in the history of the world. In three short years! The GDP was soaring. Unemployment was at the lowest we'd seen since World War II. Unemployment among blacks, Hispanics, Asians, and women was at all-time record lows. More Americans were working than at any other time in our nation's history. Real wages were growing for the first time in a decade, and entire industries like steel, aluminum, and car manufacturing had begun to come back to the United States, bringing thousands of high-quality jobs back with them. The president lifted over 2.5 million Americans, including 1.4 million children, out of poverty. His historic Tax Cuts and Jobs Act established 8,760 opportunity zones in low-income neighborhoods across the country to entice $100 billion in private investment.

Abracadabra, Barack.

Now, some of you might be thinking that pulling us out of the Covid-19 financial crash is going to be a lot harder than reversing the horrible Obama policies that held the economy back. But how is that thinking any different from Obama's? How is it any different from Joe Biden's?

Who would you rather have at the wheel during the economic storm the virus wrought? Somebody who keeps saying we're never going to make it? Or someone who's already built the economy once and assures us that we're going to be better than ever before when we get to the other side?

Thought so.

The best financial minds in the country predict a pent-up boom in our economy starting around the time this book is published. They see a rapid ascent through the third quarter of 2020 and a steady climb throughout next year. Some even say that the economy will quickly become as durable or even more robust than it was precoronavirus. As Treasury Secretary Steven Mnuchin has often said, Covid-19 was not a financial crisis, it was a medical crisis. The economy didn't crash; we shut it down. Our underlying economy, thanks to the president, was muscular enough to weather it. And it's because of that firm foundation, the experts say, that a healthy rebound waits just around the corner. Don't believe us? Look at the stock market during the shutdown. While day after day newspaper headlines screamed about unemployment numbers not seen since the Great Depression, few of them reported that in April the stock market posted its best two-week rally since the 1930s. The market hit historic highs under President Trump's leadership that few thought possible. During the Covid-19 rebound, the gains in the stock market will be limitless, as will the increases in Americans' 401(k)s and other retirement plans.

The economy will roar again under President Trump. In that roaring economy, he will continue erasing job-killing regulations. Deregulation will save Americans an estimated $50 billion next year. According to some estimates, it will create jobs by streamlining the process for companies to get projects up and running. The recently revamped guidelines for the National Environmental Policy Act are just one example of this. The old guidelines choked the life out of vital infrastructure projects such as roads, bridges, and airports with regulations. By removing them, the president is not only literally rebuilding our country's foundation but also putting hundreds of thousands of Americans back to work doing so. Private investment in infrastructure improvement is an all-around win: workers earn good, competitive salaries; businesses expand and hire more people; and Americans get roads and airports they can be proud of again.

None of this will happen, of course, if Joe Biden is elected president. The last thing America needs is a socialist administration trying to bridle an economy that wants to run. And don't kid yourself: Joe Biden would govern as the most liberal president ever elected. He has a socialist running mate who's only a heartbeat away from sitting behind the Resolute Desk. If Biden becomes president, we are going to see massive increases in taxes and spending that will blow the roof off your house. Guaranteed. They'll need the money to fund wildly bloated federal programs with hysterical climate change regulations that will cost more jobs than they generate. Which reminds us: don't think for one minute Democrats have forgotten about the Green New Deal. An editorial in the *Washington Examiner* compared the coronavirus shutdown to what life would be like under Alexandria Ocasio-Cortez's plan: "The economy is in free fall. People are miserable. Domestic abuse and mental health indicators are getting worse. But hey, at least we're almost getting the carbon reductions the green extremists say we need." Liberals were thrilled when flamingos flocked to Mumbai during the shutdown of India. It didn't matter to them that the country's unemployment rate neared 30 percent—it had flamingos!

President Trump will look to cut even more taxes in his next term. His historic 2017 tax cuts finally leveled the global playing field for the American worker. Europeans were willing to do business in America because of the Trump's pro-business climate, enabling more Americans to be hired for the first time in decades. The tax cuts also helped to lift wages, especially for those in the lowest 10 percent, helping to close the inequality gap for the first time in memory.

Next term, the president will set his sights on reducing payroll taxes, which would put more disposable income into the American workers' pockets by saving them up to 7.6 percent of their paychecks. Payroll tax cuts will also benefit employers by the same amount, giving them significant opportunities to expand and hire more people.

Look, there is no doubt that Covid-19 hit us hard. If not for the quick mitigation efforts by President Trump, we would have been in much worse shape. Contrary to what you've heard from the Fake News, his administration handled the crises decisively with this single focus: save American lives, and save America's economy. One of the policies quickly put into place was the Paycheck Protection Program. The program infused $350 billion into small businesses, loans that they didn't have to pay back if they kept their employees on the payroll.

The strong economic foundation the president built in his first term remains rock solid. From that firm foundation, second-term job growth will again reach a record-setting pace.

Clearly, the impact of the coronavirus on our economy will be seen for years to come. That is why Donald Trump must defeat Joe Biden this November. Over the past several months, the American people have witnessed "Trump Speed" up close and personal as he does everything in his power to find solutions to the coronavirus crisis and get the economy back to where it was. By contrast, Joe Biden's sleepy, defeatist approach and policies would send the US economy back to the dark ages.

Throughout his career, Biden has been looking out for himself and the family business by screwing over the forgotten men and women he claims to be fighting for. He assisted his son Hunter by putting him on Air Force Two allowing him access to trade on the family name, thus raking in millions of dollars. He allowed his brother to do basically the same thing. And now Biden wants four more years to profiteer off of hardworking Americans. We won't let that happen.

TRADE

As we mentioned, world trade is one of the most essential parts of the president's job-building policy. In the trade chapter, we outlined how the United States had a terrible trade imbalance with many countries and the president was saddled with bad trade policies such as NAFTA and the TPP. The president has played hardball with our biggest trade rivals from the get-go. Along with tax cuts, rollbacks of job-killing regulations, and the resurgence of American manufacturing, renegotiating stupid trade deals was job one for the president.

The left and Fake News divisions ridiculed President Trump when he assured them that he would put "America First" when dealing in international trade. They said he would never be able to stand up to China. But the boss saw international trade as a competitive arena with rivals who'd stop at nothing to take advantage of the United States. For him, the stakes were enormous. The president recognized that China was not only the biggest shark in the trading sea but also the one with the sharpest teeth.

While Obama was at Davos pretending to care about how China was playing dirty, Trump was telling anyone who'd listen that China should never have been let into the World Trade Organization in the first place. In his second term, you can expect the WTO to answer for its history of playing favorites, especially with China, and the organization's bias against the United States.

President Trump, you might have noticed, has the innate ability to understand the most complicated situations. He can also boil it down to the elements that are most important to the American people. To him, the facts about China were crystal clear. They'd been cheating and lying to trading partners for years. Time and again, they've manipulated the price of their currency to flood world markets with artificially low-priced goods.

The president put a stop to all of that in his first term. In his second term, he will continue to level the playing field for American workers, bringing more jobs back to the United States and demonstrating that we can compete and win against anyone when given a fair chance.

According to President Trump, the entire Chinese economy has been built on the backs of the American taxpayer. Nearly every recent president has not only allowed this to happen, but they also looked the other way while the Chinese stole our intellectual property, cheated or lied to us, and, time and again, manipulated the price of their currency. Phase 1 of the China trade deal goes a long way toward establishing parity in our trading relationship. According to the White House, Phase 2 will not only continue making the playing field with China even, it will also put a stop to the underhanded practices that China has gotten away with for years. Some of the ways Phase 2 seeks to do this is by:

- Ending Chinese cybertheft of our ideas.
- Stopping the Chinese government from subsidizing state-run enterprises that give them an unfair advantage over US companies.
- And, of paramount importance, curbing the flow of illicit fentanyl from China into the United States. The synthetic drug is the number one cause of overdose deaths and kills tens of thousands of Americans each year.

Phase 2, however, will happen only with Donald Trump in the White House. Otherwise, you can count on us reverting back to allowing the Chinese to once again dominate us in world trade.

In the second term, the Chinese coronavirus cover-up and the results of the Wuhan lab investigation will significantly impact the president's trading posture with China. The Chinese government's actions cost over a hundred thousand American lives and trillions of dollars, and the president will hold them accountable.

JUDGES

Perhaps no institution has been more transformed under the Trump administration than the federal judiciary. Nearly a quarter of all federal judges now are Trump appointees. In the next four years, expect the president to continue building on his incredible success by appointing federal judges who are constitutional conservatives and who won't legislate from the bench. In other words, he will continue to fill judicial vacancies with individuals who adhere to the constitution as intended by our Founders.

The powerful appellate courts, one step below the Supreme Court, now contain fifty Trump appointees. The average age of the Trump generation of judges is under fifty, which, with their lifetime tenure, will ensure the protection of conservative values for decades to come.

The president's most significant judicial opportunity in a second term resides in the land's highest court. Justices Ruth Bader Ginsburg and Stephen Breyer are both over eighty, and Ginsburg has been in declining health. With at least one, probably two, and possibly even three vacancies on the court in his second term, Trump will have the chance to remake the Supreme Court as no president has before him.

During the campaign, Mr. Trump promised the American people he would appoint Supreme Court justices in the mold of the great Antonin Scalia. He kept that promise with the appointment of justices Gorsuch and Kavanaugh. In a second term, he will completely remake the court in a way that even Justice Scalia couldn't have imagined. The justices he appoints will champion pro-life, pro-family, and pro-faith values and render judicial opinions that will be the law of the land for generations.

For this to happen, of course, we need to also retain a Republican majority in the Senate. Only then will we be able to fend off the left's unscrupulous attacks, such as the one perpetrated against Brett Kavanaugh. The crazed left in the Senate almost destroyed an exemplary judge's career. It brought excruciating pain to his young family, all for power and politics. The same radicals who demanded accusers with unproven allegations be believed at face value are now silent when it comes to Tara Reade and her corroborated claims against Joe Biden. The hypocrisy of senators Chuck Schumer, Kirsten Gillibrand, Dianne Feinstein, et al., knows no bounds. If not for Justice Kavanaugh's courage and moral strength, the Democrats would have driven him from the public square. The Kavanaugh fight was just the beginning. The liberal left will stop at nothing to disparage, destroy, and denigrate qualified conservative jurists from serving on the high court. A more establishment president would have caved to the onslaught of attacks on Judge Kavanaugh and would have likely pulled his nomination; not Donald Trump. As usual, he doubled down to ensure that a good man's life wasn't ruined.

IMMIGRATION

A strong federal judiciary, especially on the Supreme Court, will strengthen President Trump's already bold merit-based immigration policies.

The Trump administration has replaced hundreds of miles of Obama's chain-link fence along the US-Mexico border with massive steel barriers and built a new big, beautiful, high-tech wall along hundreds of additional miles. Over two hundred miles of wall have already been built, and by next term, there will be hundreds of additional miles of wall on our southern border.

The left in Congress, as well as immigration activists, have fought President Trump's immigration policies at every turn.

They have litigated all the way to the Supreme Court on multiple occasions, using the federal judiciary as a weapon to block executive orders. This activism slowed the administration's efforts. But now that the president has prevailed in every case, he is once again moving at Trump Speed to finish building the wall.

In his first term, the president signed an executive order banning travel into the United States from certain terror-supporting countries like Iran, Libya, and Syria, to name a few. In a second term, expect President Trump to continue policies that will keep Americans safe.

In his first term, he empowered Immigration and Customs Enforcement (ICE) to carry out systematic raids and open immigrant detention centers all over the country.

Next term, he will expand ICE so it will be able to better carry out its mission of weeding out criminal immigrants who cost the American taxpayer a minimum $150 billion a year. The president will also use every legal strategy at his disposal to go after sanctuary cities that harbor these criminals. Last year, an appellate court ruled that the Department of Justice could withhold funds from cities that hide undocumented immigrants. With a Supreme Court that sides with the administration's constitutional position, look for President Trump to deconstruct these havens for illegal immigration.

Last year, the Trump administration began the Remain in Mexico policy on our southern border. The new policy requires migrants from Mexico and other Latin American countries who claim asylum in the United States to wait in Mexico while US immigration judges decide their case. The program it replaced, the Migrant Protection Protocols, allowed migrants crossing the border illegally to wait in the United States for their cases to be heard. Under the old policy,

an illegal immigrant would be given a number with "a promise" to return to court when it was their turn. It was called the
"catch-and-release" policy because it depended on the migrant
returning to the court to have a hearing. In truth, most of them
simply disappeared because they were already in the United
States! The program permitted hundreds of thousands of illegal immigrants to disappear into American communities.

With four more years, President Trump will expand his
"America First" policies of border protection and the removal
of criminal aliens. And of course, he'll finish his big, beautiful
wall, ensuring our borders are permanently secure.

FOREIGN POLICY

In the president's second term, both US foreign policy and
our military will be stronger. As we've mentioned, with his
strong position on NATO, the president has already won
concessions. Germany and many other member nations are
already paying more, as they should, and American taxpayers are paying less. President Trump does not intend to stop
there. He won't rest until each member of the alliance pays
their fair share. The days of the United States footing NATO's
bill is over—that is, if the president is reelected.

President Trump will continue his hard-line stance against
Iran with sanctions and swift justice. Just ask Iran's blood-
thirsty general Qassim Suleimani how quick Donald Trump's
justice is. Oh, that's right. You can't because he's dead. Unlike
Obama's infamous "red line" in Syria, the Iranian government knows not to push this president. President Trump did
what weak Obama couldn't do: he defeated the deadly caliph-
ate and decimated ISIS in short order. In his second term, he
will continue to fight the enemy on their soil not ours.

Look, Donald J. Trump is a businessman. He goes about his duties as president as a businessman would. And like a good businessman, he's not going to allow the United States to be taken for a ride. He's not going to let NATO members get away with not paying their fair share. He's going to stop the trillion-dollar money drain and the unnecessary loss of American lives in the unending wars in Iraq and Afghanistan. As he said in his State of the Union address, it's not America's job to serve as other nations' law enforcement agencies. He is going to continue pulling us from treaties and deals that don't put "America First," no matter how the politics of it looks. Take Japan, for example. Right now, there are more than fifty thousand US troops stationed there, including nearly thirty thousand at our base on Okinawa. For that privilege, Japan pays us a comparatively measly amount of $2 billion a year. Right after World War II, the deal we made with Japan might have been prudent to our interest. But seventy years later, it makes no sense at all. The agreement expires in March 2021, and President Trump has already told Japan he wants them to pay four times what they're paying now to keep American troops stationed there. If you think Joe Biden would demand the price our troops are worth, you've been spending too much time in your basement like him.

The world has seen President Trump's resolve to achieve peace through strength and knows he is willing to do whatever it takes to protect Americans' vital national interests.

THE MILITARY

In 1991, Secretary of Defense Dick Cheney called Ronald Reagan and thanked the former president for the strong military he'd left for the new administration. In the wake of the weak president Jimmy Carter, Reagan fought communism and rightly saw the need to build the United States' armed forces into the greatest fighting machine the world has ever seen.

There's a lot of Ronald Reagan in Donald Trump.

During his first four years in office, the president has spent more than $2.2 trillion strengthening our military. The Pentagon has ordered ninety stealth F-35s, the most advanced fighting machine in the world. He has funded a massive buildup of our naval fleet. New ballistic submarines with cutting-edge 5G technology are now being built. Obama had put our military machine into mothballs. A priority for President Trump was restoring its readiness and capability. Under his direction, our military received new training, improved maintenance of equipment, and a restocking of depleted munitions. The increase in military spending has been more than the entire military budget of any other country except China. With Donald Trump as president, no one will have a stronger military than we will.

Maybe his biggest move in strengthening our military, however, came in December 2019. It was then that the president signed legislation forming a space force. It was the first time since Harry Truman created the air force that a new branch of the armed forces was formed. Almost immediately, liberals and the Fake News tried to turn the space force into a joke with comparisons to Mr. Spock and Captain Picard. You didn't see many people in China and Russia laughing, however. Maybe that's because they already have their own versions of a space force. Military experts agree that future battlefields will exist hundreds of miles above the earth's surface. Today, there are literally thousands of US satellites orbiting the earth. They control everything from GPS and package delivery to missile guidance and defense. Our enemies are close to having the capability to turn those satellites off permanently, which would severely damage our economy and way of life. During a war, the price would be even steeper. Imagine shutting down satellites that communicate troop movements or detect missile launches!

But the posture of the space force won't be only defensive. With it, we will gain the upper hand over satellites that pose a risk to the United States. When it comes to war, space really is the final frontier. With his vision and strong love of our country, President Trump made that bold move to keep future generations of Americans safe.

As they did with Ronald Reagan, our enemies have watched firsthand as President Trump has rebuilt our military once again into the most powerful the world has ever seen. And as in Reagan's time, the improvement and expansion of our strengthened military will keep the United States in that vaunted place for years to come.

––––––––––––

With Donald Trump as our president, America can hold her head up high on the world stage. He's brought back the swagger to our military, saved us billions of dollars on unnecessary expenditures, and made us safer. But he also knows there is much more to do and that all of the gains we have made can be wiped out if Joe Biden is elected president.

So the choice is stark: either we can revert back to a do-nothing Democrat administration, erasing all the gains we've made over the last four years to return to the stagnant, failed policies that held us back for much too long, or we can let President Trump lead us forward and build on his gains. We are literally at the point of no return: either we turn around in defeat, or we give Donald Trump the time to rocket us to a fourth dimension. As the president said about the economy, "I built it once; I'll build it a second time."

So, yes, this is the most important election of our lifetime. And it's an easy choice to make.

BACK IN THE SADDLE

We built the greatest economy the world has ever seen, and we're going to do it again.

President Trump, 2020 Trump for President
campaign ad, May 3, 2020

O n October 25, 1995, the *New York Times* published an article entitled "Crowning the Comeback King." The story was about a luncheon in Manhattan honoring Donald J. Trump. At the time, Mr. Trump had refinanced his casinos in Atlantic City with a set of ingenious deals that had taken them out of the red and turned them into money-making machines again. He had also survived a collapse of the Manhattan real estate market, one that ruined titans of the industry. While most of the New York City real estate market lay idle, he announced he was building a new condominium and hotel overlooking Central Park and a seventeen-building complex on the West Side of Manhattan, much to the chagrin of leftist Jerrold Nadler, the congressman from the district, who had fought the project for years. Personally, the boss had gone from being billions of dollars in the red to being a billion in the black.

So incredible was Mr. Trump's comeback it was listed in *Guinness World Records*. It really was. At the luncheon, the "limousine king" Bill Fugazy, a pal of George Steinbrenner and Roy Cohn, handed Mr. Trump a glass-encased boomerang. "You throw it, and it always comes back," he said. Maybe the most remarkable part of Donald Trump's comeback, however, was that he himself predicted it.

According to one Trump biographer, at the depth of his financial troubles, Mr. Trump told an associate that he would again be on the cover of *Time* magazine as the "comeback of the century." Then he told *The Sunday Times* of London that he was going to be bigger than ever.

Of course, that was exactly what happened. In 1997, he wrote a book about it, *The Art of the Comeback*. During the 2016 campaign, we saw for ourselves how Donald Trump made comebacks into an art form.

Remember when candidate Trump's remarks about Senator John McCain had supposedly sunk his campaign? Every news reporter with a computer was tapping out stories saying that Trump was out of the race. The *New York Post* headline read "Don Voyage!"

What happened? His poll numbers went up.

Then there was the *Access Hollywood* tape. Remember? The establishment in the Republican Party begun to jump ship after that one.

What happened? He went out and crushed Hillary in a nationally televised debate.

Then came the greatest comeback of them all. In the days and weeks leading up to election day, every elite liberal news outlet was predicting the drubbing that awaited Donald Trump. The *New York Times*' "The Upshot" gave Hillary an 85 percent chance of winning. Deadspin said that Trump "was going to get his ass kicked." The *Washington Post* wrote that his chances were "approaching zero."

Hmmm. Wonder how that turned out.

So you would think that the squawking heads of MSDNC, the *New York Times*, and the Democrat-Socialist Party would have learned its lesson, right?

Nope.

As is historically the case around this time, the media always counts out the Republican incumbent. Way back in July 1988, the *New York Times* published a poll showing Massachusetts governor Michael Dukakis leading Vice President George H. W. Bush by a margin of 55 to 38 percent. By the spring of 2020, the liberal press was counting President Trump out again. Though polling for his reelection was mixed and even strong in some battleground states, you'd never have known it by the way the press was reporting it. "Biden Leads Trump by Double Digits in New National Poll," MSNBC shouted. "Biden's Lead over Trump Widens—but Strain on His Virtual Campaign Grows," *The Guardian* blared. Battleground-state polling had "Biden's Campaign Swaggering," read *Politico*.

If we didn't know any better, we would swear they were talking about Hillary all over again.

Though the inaccuracies in the reporting were frustrating, it was nothing new. What really frustrated us was that the physical campaign, for the most part, was still on lockdown. By May, we were ready to jump out of our shoes we were so eager to hit the trail. We knew, of course, that the old idea of "retail campaigning" didn't exist anymore. But we weren't going to sit around crying about how unfair the world was. We knew we had to adapt, and we came up with some great ideas for the campaign to work around the coronavirus. We were anxious to tell the president about them. As it happened, the president wanted to talk with us too.

"Where've you been?" the Boss asked Corey on the phone. "Come in and see me."

———————

During the meeting, the president called Johnny McEntee into the Oval Office. Having people around whom he knows well and trusts always puts him at ease. That's especially true with those of us who were with him during the incredible ride of the 2016 election. When you go through an experience like that campaign together, you form an unbreakable, unshakable bond. We began talking about others who have stayed loyal to him from the beginning. Some of those names you know: Dan Scavino, Stephen Miller, Cassidy Dumbauld. But there are plenty of others who are as dedicated as we are but have never been in the spotlight.

It was while thinking of those unheralded people that Thomas Tsaveras came to mind. If you want to know how believing in Donald Trump can change your life, there's no better example.

A mere twenty-three years old today, Thomas had a clear idea of what he wanted out of life and the determination to achieve it. Corey remembers the first time he met him. Thomas got himself to Trump Tower and marched into the campaign office.

"I love Donald Trump," he told Corey. "I want to volunteer for the campaign."

"You're hired," Corey answered. "Get to work."

There's a famous photo of Mr. and Mrs. Trump stepping onto the golden escalator in Trump Tower on the day he announced he was running for president. In the photo you can see Thomas standing behind the future president wearing a "Make America Great Again" T-shirt, a big smile on his face.

After the president was elected, Dave made sure Thomas was part of the transition team and asked him if he wanted to go to work in Washington, DC. In March 2017, Thomas got word he was going to work in the White House. It was a dream come true!

Though he is loved and respected throughout Trump land, Thomas owns a special place in Corey's heart. Back on Easter 2017, Corey and his family were invited to the White House for the egg roll. At the time, John Kelly was the chief of staff, and he told Corey that he wasn't allowed on the White House grounds without an escort. Kelly's decree could have made the visit, which the whole Lewandowski family was looking forward to, tense and unpleasant. As luck would have it, Thomas was assigned as his escort. He took Corey and the family to the Truman Bowling Alley in the basement of the Eisenhower Executive Office Building, where he let them bowl as long as they wanted to on the most exclusive lanes in the world.

After Corey told the story, President Trump had Molly Michael call Thomas to tell him that the president wanted to see him in the Oval Office. We could only imagine what went through Thomas's mind when he answered the call. He was at the door of the Oval Office in the blink of an eye. The president chatted with him for a few minutes, thanked him for his dedication, and then took a photo with him standing behind the Resolute Desk.

"You keep it up, Thomas, you're gonna be the chief of staff of this place," Corey said to the young man whose grin could have swallowed his ears.

"You never know," the president said with a smile. "You just never know."

When the president sent for us in May, there were a few people in line to enter the temporary medical station outside the West Wing. Once inside the tent, we encountered a small team of medical staffers. One pointed a noncontact thermometer at our forehead to take our temperature, while another asked us if we'd been out of the country in the last thirty days. Additionally, they asked a series of medical-related questions, inquiring whether we had had flulike symptoms. Once it was determined we didn't have a fever and weren't recently out of the country, the team directed us through security. On the other side of the checkpoint, a young woman named Lili Hernandez from Molly's office met us and escorted us to be tested for Covid-19. Along with the trauma units, the White House medical staff has a series of examination rooms in the basement of the Eisenhower Executive Office Building. That's where we headed.

Just outside the reception area was a small table with dozens of medical-grade surgical masks, the ones every person had to wear while on the White House complex. The antechamber of the exam room gave us the impression that we'd walked into a waiting room at a normal doctor's office. There were chairs in which to sit, and behind a window there were medical staff, who asked us several more questions and gave us some forms to fill out. Inside the examination room, however, things were a little different from your average doctor's office. For one, the examination chair was royal blue and imprinted with the presidential seal. Corey went in first. He settled into the blue seat, asked for a Teddy bear, and then held on to the chair for dear life.

Though he actually did ask for a Teddy bear, he didn't have to grip the arms at all. It was our first Covid-19 test, and we had heard that they pushed a probe all the way up your nasal canal into your cranium. That was unsettling to us to say the least. The medical staff in the examination room, however, assured us that the test they were giving wasn't nearly as invasive. They used what is known as the Abbott fifteen-minute test, which swabbed only the nasal passage. The test took a couple of seconds, and just like that, we were on our way. We'd given the unit our contact information ahead of time and were told that we would be contacted if the test was positive. Having a little time to kill, we visited Johnny McEntee and Brian Jack, both of whom have offices in the EEOB.

Twenty minutes later and Covid-19 free, we headed to see the president.

At the entrance to the West Wing, we ran into Andrew Giuliani and chatted with him for a few minutes. A former Division I college golfer, Andrew asked Dave about Griffin's game. Two weeks later, on Memorial Day weekend, he would see for himself. Along with PGA golfer Bobby Hurley, Andrew and Dave's seventeen-year-old son played a round at nearby Trump National Golf Club. Oh, yeah, they also picked up a fourth: the guy who owns the course.

Under enormous pressure of playing with President Trump, Griffin shot a 78 and so impressed the president with his game and maturity that the boss would personally call Dave the next morning to lavish effusive praise on the young man. What brings this story full circle is that Trump National was the site of the Children's National Medical Center charity event, which Dave ran with his buddy Mike Murray for many years and which Mr. Trump began supporting back in 2010. Children's was one of the hospitals where Griffin was operated on. It was during the run-up to the charity event that Dave first met Donald Trump. Dave had flown out to Las Vegas to talk with casino magnate Steve Wynn about donating some prizes for his charity event. Frank Luntz, the architect of Newt Gingrich's Contract with America, had introduced Dave to Wynn, who is politically active. When Steve asked him where the event was being held, Dave told him Lowes Island Club, just outside Washington, DC.

"My friend Donald Trump owns that course!" Steve said.

The boss had just bought Lowes Island Club, which he would upgrade and then rename Trump National. Over a conference call, Wynn introduced Dave to Mr. Trump, who said he'd be happy to donate to the good cause. Not only did the boss give generous gifts to be raffled off, he donated money and then took Dave to lunch at the Trump Grill in Trump Tower. It was at that lunch when he first picked Dave's brain about politics.

Like the last scene of *Casablanca*, it was the beginning of a beautiful friendship.

Andrew walked with us into the West Wing lobby, where Mark Meadows came out to greet us. Because of Covid-19, we had not seen Mark since he assumed the role as White House chief of staff, and we were surprised when he popped his head into the lobby and said, "Hey, fellas, come on with me." After a handshake-free greeting, Mark instructed us to follow him back to the chief of staff's office.

"Mark," Corey said wryly. "You're the fourth chief of staff, we know where we're going."

Dave and Mark Meadows go way back. When Mark was a brand-new congressman and founding member of the House Freedom Caucus, he had made a bold move to challenge House speaker John Boehner. Though bold, the move didn't get a lot of traction. As we sat in the chief of staff's office, Mark reminded us that Dave was the only conservative who met with him during that time. Dave and Citizens United have always strongly supported Meadows.

After a brief chat, the chief of staff walked us down the hall to the Oval Office. As we entered the famous room, we saw, sitting near the fireplace, our old pal and current deputy chief of staff for communications, Dan Scavino. He was looking at his cell phone, on which he had the "Loser" video of Mitt Romney playing.

"Have you seen it?" the president asked from behind the Resolute Desk.

The video, which went viral, shows a montage of both Romney and Donald Trump on their respective election nights. It's actually pretty funny.

We noticed right away that the chairs inside the famous office were set with social distancing in mind. We took our usual seats in front of the president's desk.

After some friendly banter, the president asked, as he always does, about our families. Next, he turned to business. He asked us how the campaign was doing. We then went over the publicly available polling state by state. We had done our homework and were frank in our assessments. In total, as we've said, the polling results were a mixed bag, but we gave him both the good and bad news. Our relationship with the boss is such that we can have honest conversations with him. He appreciated our forthright evaluation, but we could see the wheels turning in his head. When you've been with Donald Trump on a daily basis for an extended period of time, as we both had been on the campaign, you know when he puts his game face on, he's ready for battle. The expression he showed wasn't anger—believe us, we've seen that look before—it was determination.

"Look at it this way, sir," Dave said, "you're in a lot better shape than you were this time in 2016."

As part of our discussion we recommended some big, strategic ideas. One was a suggestion that the president challenge Joe Biden to additional debates. Traditionally, there are three presidential candidate debates and one vice presidential debate scheduled by the nonpartisan Presidential Debate Commission. The commission picks the location, the networks, and moderators and sets the rules of each debate. The problem is with early voting, mail-in voting, and absentee ballots, tens of millions of votes will be cast before the first scheduled debate. With additional debates, the American people who vote early will get to see the stark differences between the president and Sleepy Joe Biden. And no doubt they'll see for themselves that the former vice president is not mentally up to the job.

Additional debates, we told the president, are a win-win situation.

"If Biden says no, he comes across as weak," Corey said. "And if he agrees to the debates, well . . ." He didn't finish the sentence. Dave did. "You'll tear his face off," he said.

Plus, we said, it will be a ratings bonanza.

The president really liked the idea, but we were only getting started. We told him the campaign needed to be in an offensive mode. Bring the fight to Biden, we said. Covid-19 hasn't changed everything. Define your opponent before he defines you. The 2016 campaign had had the energy of a nuclear reactor, with candidate Trump outworking crooked Hillary every day. We told him he needed to have high-energy people around him to re-create the force of 2016.

Using innovative opportunities, we recommended he get back out on the road and speak directly to the American people. It's no secret that President Trump was frustrated that the virus had put a stop to his travel. We were, too. Rallies are the beating heart of Donald Trump's political machine. We had to get them started again. But that meant doing some out-of-the-box thinking while still keeping people safe. For the president, health and safety are paramount.

But most of all, we said, the American people want to be reminded that he is outworking Biden every day—by a lot. The reelection effort is a harder race than 2016, we told him. This time, you're not just running against the Democrat Party but an elite liberal media apparatus that has been building to this moment for the past four years. This time there would be no element of surprise. The way to overcome that was to

remind the American people not only of your own indefatigable spirit but, by contrast, show them that Biden's not only
mentally incapable but also physically inadequate too.

By the expression the president wore, we could tell he
wanted to accelerate his campaign activities immediately.
Though he fully understands the limitations of the pandemic,
he had the look that told us he wanted the old gang to saddle
up and ride again.

We exchanged glances with each other. Both of us thought
the same thing: Giddy-up!

As we walked out of the Oval Office that day, somehow we
knew we were going to get through this pandemic and be better on the other side. Our years with the president have been
marked by ups and downs. It's been a constant fight against
our combined enemies who only want to see the president fail.
But each time they hit us, we hit back harder. We will never
stop fighting for what's right. We learned that from the man
we just left.

Like Thomas Tsaveras, we also knew that we had the best
jobs of our lives: helping the president get reelected. By the
time this book hits the shelves, there will be just weeks until
election day. We already gave you plenty of concrete reasons
to reelect President Donald Trump. But if you want to know
why you should reelect him, just ask Thomas—or any of the
other tens of millions of people whose lives he's changed for
the better.

As we write this, the nation is reopening slowly and
methodically. Testing for Covid-19 has been supercharged,
and the president's dedication to finding a cure is bringing
a vaccine ever closer. His "Do it all, do it now" mentality, in
conjunction with public-private partnerships, has created the

environment for the American people to get back to work and once again be the envy of the world.

If you need proof that Donald Trump loves a comeback, just look at what he's already been able to do for the country. On June 8, a little more than a hundred days since the first cases of Covid-19 appeared in the United States, the stock market completely recovered all the losses that had happened since we were forced to shut down our economy to save lives. As protests raged in the streets and the president's enemies attacked him from all sides, his strategy of being careful about the virus while pushing states to reopen paid dividends   both for him and for the country.

In every stage of his life—as a businessman, as a political candidate, and as president of the United States—Donald J. Trump has shown his ability to stage comebacks against the most incredible odds. His story is one that could only happen in America, the land of comebacks. We now face perhaps the most important chapter in our country's history. We can either follow our president, meet and overcome these challenges, or shirk from them and let those who don't mind losing lead the way.

No words can adequately describe the indominable spirit of the American people. The combination of this country's unbreakable will led by a president who refuses to lose makes us invincible.

And will allow us to write the greatest American comeback story of them all.

Four More Years!

APPENDIX A

PRESIDENT TRUMP'S SPEECH AT MOUNT RUSHMORE

July 3, 2020

WELL, THANK YOU VERY MUCH. And Governor Noem, Secretary Bernhardt—very much appreciate it—members of Congress, distinguished guests, and a very special hello to South Dakota.

As we begin this Fourth of July weekend, the First Lady and I wish each and every one of you a very, very Happy Independence Day. Thank you.

Let us show our appreciation to the South Dakota Army and Air National Guard, and the U.S. Air Force for inspiring us with that magnificent display of American air power, and of course, our gratitude, as always, to the legendary and very talented Blue Angels. Thank you very much.

Let us also send our deepest thanks to our wonderful veterans, law enforcement, first responders, and the doctors, nurses, and scientists working tirelessly to kill the virus. They're working hard. I want to thank them very, very much.

We're grateful as well to your state's Congressional delegation: Senators John Thune—John, thank you very much. Senator Mike Rounds, thank you, Mike—and Dusty Johnson, Congressman. Hi, Dusty. Thank you. And all others with us tonight from Congress, thank you very much for coming. We appreciate it.

There could be no better place to celebrate America's independence than beneath this magnificent, incredible, majestic mountain and monument to the greatest Americans who have ever lived.

Today, we pay tribute to the exceptional lives and extraordinary legacies of George Washington, Thomas Jefferson, Abraham Lincoln, and Teddy Roosevelt. I am here as your President to proclaim before the country and before the world: This monument will never be desecrated, these heroes will never be defaced, their legacy will never, ever be destroyed, their achievements will never be forgotten, and Mount Rushmore will stand forever as an eternal tribute to our forefathers and to our freedom.

We gather tonight to herald the most important day in the history of nations: July 4th, 1776. At those words, every American heart should swell with pride. Every American family should cheer with delight. And every American patriot should be filled with joy, because each of you lives in the most magnificent country in the history of the world, and it will soon be greater than ever before.

Our Founders launched not only a revolution in government, but a revolution in the pursuit of justice, equality, liberty, and prosperity. No nation has done more to advance the human condition than the United States of America. And no people have done more to promote human progress than the citizens of our great nation.

It was all made possible by the courage of 56 patriots who gathered in Philadelphia 244 years ago and signed the Declaration of Independence. They enshrined a divine truth that changed the world forever when they said: ". . . all men are created equal."

These immortal words set in motion the unstoppable march of freedom. Our Founders boldly declared that we are all endowed with the same divine rights—given [to] us by our Creator in Heaven. And that which God has given us, we will allow no one, ever, to take away—ever.

Seventeen seventy-six represented the culmination of thousands of years of western civilization and the triumph not only of spirit, but of wisdom, philosophy, and reason.

And yet, as we meet here tonight, there is a growing danger that threatens every blessing our ancestors fought so hard for, struggled, they bled to secure.

Our nation is witnessing a merciless campaign to wipe out our history, defame our heroes, erase our values, and indoctrinate our children.

Angry mobs are trying to tear down statues of our Founders, deface our most sacred memorials, and unleash a wave of violent crime in our cities. Many of these people have no idea why they are doing this, but some know exactly what they are doing. They think the American people are weak and soft and submissive. But no, the American people are strong and proud, and they will not allow our country, and all of its values, history, and culture, to be taken from them.

One of their political weapons is "Cancel Culture"—driving people from their jobs, shaming dissenters, and demanding total submission from anyone who disagrees. This is the very definition of totalitarianism, and it is completely alien to our culture and our values, and it has absolutely no place in the United States of America. This attack on our liberty, our magnificent liberty, must be stopped, and it will be stopped very quickly. We will expose this dangerous movement, protect our nation's children, end this radical assault, and preserve our beloved American way of life.

In our schools, our newsrooms, even our corporate boardrooms, there is a new far-left fascism that demands absolute allegiance. If you do not speak its language, perform its rituals, recite its mantras, and follow its commandments, then you will be censored, banished, blacklisted, persecuted, and punished. It's not going to happen to us.

Make no mistake: this left-wing cultural revolution is designed to overthrow the American Revolution. In so doing, they would destroy the very civilization that rescued billions from poverty, disease, violence, and hunger, and that lifted humanity to new heights of achievement, discovery, and progress.

To make this possible, they are determined to tear down every statue, symbol, and memory of our national heritage.

That is why I am deploying federal law enforcement to protect our monuments, arrest the rioters, and prosecute offenders to the fullest extent of the law.

I am pleased to report that yesterday, federal agents arrested the suspected ringleader of the attack on the statue of Andrew Jackson in Washington, D.C. and, in addition, hundreds more have been arrested.

Under the executive order I signed last week—pertaining to the Veterans' Memorial Preservation and Recognition Act and other laws—people who damage or deface federal statues or monuments will get a minimum of 10 years in prison. And obviously, that includes our beautiful Mount Rushmore.

Our people have a great memory. They will never forget the destruction of statues and monuments to George Washington, Abraham Lincoln, Ulysses S. Grant, abolitionists, and many others.

The violent mayhem we have seen in the streets of cities that are run by liberal Democrats, in every case, is the predictable result of years of extreme indoctrination and bias in education, journalism, and other cultural institutions.

Against every law of society and nature, our children are taught in school to hate their own country, and to believe that the men and women who built it were not heroes, but [they] were villains. The radical view of American history is a web of lies—all perspective is removed, every virtue is obscured, every motive is twisted, every fact is distorted, and every flaw is magnified until the history is purged and the record is disfigured beyond all recognition.

This movement is openly attacking the legacies of every person on Mount Rushmore. They defile the memory of Washington, Jefferson, Lincoln, and Roosevelt. Today, we will set history and history's record straight.

Before these figures were immortalized in stone, they were American giants in full flesh and blood, gallant men whose intrepid deeds unleashed the greatest leap of human advancement the world has ever known. Tonight, I will tell you and, most importantly, the youth of our nation, the true stories of these great, great men.

From head to toe, George Washington represented the strength, grace, and dignity of the American people. From a small volunteer force of citizen farmers, he created the Continental Army out of nothing and rallied them to stand against the most powerful military on Earth.

Through eight long years, through the brutal winter at Valley Forge, through setback after setback on the field of battle, he led those patriots to ultimate triumph. When the Army had dwindled to a few thousand men at Christmas of 1776, when defeat seemed absolutely certain, he took what remained of his forces on a daring nighttime crossing of the Delaware River.

They marched through nine miles of frigid darkness, many without boots on their feet, leaving a trail of blood in the snow. In the morning, they seized victory at Trenton. After forcing the surrender of the most powerful empire on the planet at Yorktown, General Washington did not claim power, but simply returned to Mount Vernon as a private citizen.

When called upon again, he presided over the Constitutional Convention in Philadelphia, and was unanimously elected our first President. When he stepped down after two terms, his former adversary King George called him "the greatest man of the age." He remains first in our hearts to this day. For as long as Americans love this land, we will honor and cherish the father of our country, George Washington. He will never be removed, abolished, and most of all, he will never be forgotten.

Thomas Jefferson—the great Thomas Jefferson—was 33 years old when he traveled north to Pennsylvania and brilliantly authored one of the greatest treasures of human history, the Declaration of Independence. He also drafted Virginia's constitution, and conceived and wrote the Virginia Statute for Religious Freedom, a model for our cherished First Amendment.

After serving as the first Secretary of State, and then Vice President, he was elected to the Presidency. He ordered American warriors to crush the Barbary pirates, he doubled the size of our nation with the Louisiana Purchase, and he sent the famous explorers Lewis and Clark into the west on a daring expedition to the Pacific Ocean.

He was an architect, an inventor, a diplomat, a scholar, the founder of one of the world's great universities, and an ardent defender of liberty. Americans will forever admire the author of American freedom, Thomas Jefferson. And he, too, will never, ever be abandoned by us.

Abraham Lincoln, the savior of our union, was a self-taught country lawyer who grew up in a log cabin on the American frontier.

The first Republican President, he rose to high office from obscurity, based on a force and clarity of his anti-slavery convictions. Very, very strong convictions.

He signed the law that built the Transcontinental Railroad; he signed the Homestead Act, given to some incredible scholars—as simply defined, ordinary citizens free land to settle anywhere in the American West; and he led the country through the darkest hours of American history, giving every ounce of strength that he had to ensure that government of the people, by the people, and for the people did not perish from this Earth.

He served as Commander-in-Chief of the U.S. Armed Forces during our bloodiest war, the struggle that saved our union and extinguished the evil of slavery. Over 600,000 died in that war; more than 20,000 were killed or wounded in a single day at Antietam. At Gettysburg, 157 years ago, the Union bravely withstood an assault of nearly 15,000 men and threw back Pickett's charge.

Lincoln won the Civil War; he issued the Emancipation Proclamation; he led the passage of the 13th Amendment, abolishing slavery for all time and ultimately, his determination to preserve our nation and our union cost him his life. For as long as we live, Americans will uphold and revere the immortal memory of President Abraham Lincoln.

Theodore Roosevelt exemplified the unbridled confidence of our national culture and identity. He saw the towering grandeur of America's mission in the world and he pursued it with overwhelming energy and zeal.

As a Lieutenant Colonel during the Spanish-American War, he led the famous Rough Riders to defeat the enemy at San Juan Hill. He cleaned up corruption as Police Commissioner of New York City, then served as the Governor of New York, Vice President, and at 42 years old, became the youngest-ever President of the United States.

He sent our great new naval fleet around the globe to announce America's arrival as a world power. He gave us many of our national parks, including the Grand Canyon; he oversaw the construction of the awe-inspiring Panama Canal; and he is the only person ever awarded both the Nobel Peace Prize and the Congressional Medal of Honor. He was American freedom personified in full. The American people will never relinquish the bold, beautiful, and untamed spirit of Theodore Roosevelt.

No movement that seeks to dismantle these treasured American legacies can possibly have a love of America at its heart. Can't have it. No person who remains quiet at the destruction of this resplendent heritage can possibly lead us to a better future.

The radical ideology attacking our country advances under the banner of social justice. But in truth, it would demolish both justice and society. It would transform justice into an instrument of division and vengeance, and it would turn our free and inclusive society into a place of repression, domination, and exclusion.

They want to silence us, but we will not be silenced.

We will state the truth in full, without apology: We declare that the United States of America is the most just and exceptional nation ever to exist on Earth.

We are proud of the fact that our country was founded on Judeo-Christian principles, and we understand that these values have dramatically advanced the cause of peace and justice throughout the world.

We know that the American family is the bedrock of American life.

We recognize the solemn right and moral duty of every nation to secure its borders. And we are building the wall.

We remember that governments exist to protect the safety and happiness of their own people. A nation must care for its own citizens first. We must take care of America first. It's time.

We believe in equal opportunity, equal justice, and equal treatment for citizens of every race, background, religion, and creed. Every child, of every color—born and unborn—is made in the holy image of God.

We want free and open debate, not speech codes and cancel culture.

We embrace tolerance, not prejudice.

We support the courageous men and women of law enforcement. We will never abolish our police or our great Second Amendment, which gives us the right to keep and bear arms.

We believe that our children should be taught to love their country, honor our history, and respect our great American flag.

We stand tall, we stand proud, and we only kneel to Almighty God.

This is who we are. This is what we believe. And these are the values that will guide us as we strive to build an even better and greater future.

Those who seek to erase our heritage want Americans to forget our pride and our great dignity, so that we can no longer understand ourselves or America's destiny. In toppling the heroes of 1776, they seek to dissolve the bonds of love and loyalty that we feel for our country, and that we feel for each other. Their goal is not a better America, their goal is the end of America.

In its place, they want power for themselves. But just as patriots did in centuries past, the American people will stand in their way—and we will win, and win quickly and with great dignity.

We will never let them rip America's heroes from our monuments, or from our hearts. By tearing down Washington and Jefferson, these radicals would tear down the very heritage for which men gave their lives to win the Civil War;

they would erase the memory that inspired those soldiers to go to their deaths, singing these words of the Battle Hymn of the Republic: "As He died to make men Holy, let us die to make men free, while God is marching on."

They would tear down the principles that propelled the abolition of slavery in America and, ultimately, around the world, ending an evil institution that had plagued humanity for thousands and thousands of years. Our opponents would tear apart the very documents that Martin Luther King used to express his dream, and the ideas that were the foundation of the righteous movement for Civil Rights. They would tear down the beliefs, culture, and identity that have made America the most vibrant and tolerant society in the history of the Earth.

My fellow Americans, it is time to speak up loudly and strongly and powerfully and defend the integrity of our country.

It is time for our politicians to summon the bravery and determination of our American ancestors. It is time. It is time to plant our flag and protect the greatest of this nation, for citizens of every race, in every city, and every part of this glorious land. For the sake of our honor, for the sake of our children, for the sake of our union, we must protect and preserve our history, our heritage, and our great heroes.

Here tonight, before the eyes of our forefathers, Americans declare again, as we did 244 years ago: that we will not be tyrannized, we will not be demeaned, and we will not be intimidated by bad, evil people. It will not happen.

We will proclaim the ideals of the Declaration of Independence, and we will never surrender the spirit and the courage and the cause of July 4th, 1776.

Upon this ground, we will stand firm and unwavering. In the face of lies meant to divide us, demoralize us, and diminish us, we will show that the story of America unites us, inspires us, includes us all, and makes everyone free.

We must demand that our children are taught once again to see America as did Reverend Martin Luther King, when he said that the Founders had signed "a promissory note" to every future generation. Dr. King saw that the mission of justice required us to fully embrace our founding ideals. Those ideals are so important to us—the founding ideals. He called on his fellow citizens not to rip down their heritage, but to live up to their heritage.

Above all, our children, from every community, must be taught that to be American is to inherit the spirit of the most adventurous and confident people ever to walk the face of the Earth.

Americans are the people who pursued our Manifest Destiny across the ocean, into the uncharted wilderness, over the tallest mountains, and then into the skies and even into the stars.

We are the country of Andrew Jackson, Ulysses S. Grant, and Frederick Douglass. We are the land of Wild Bill Hickock and Buffalo Bill Cody. We are the nation that gave rise to the Wright Brothers, the Tuskegee Airmen, Harriet Tubman, Clara Barton, Jesse Owens, George Patton—General George Patton—the great Louie Armstrong, Alan Shepard, Elvis Presley, and Mohammad Ali. And only America could have produced them all. No other place.

We are the culture that put up the Hoover Dam, laid down the highways, and sculpted the skyline of Manhattan. We are the people who dreamed a spectacular dream—it was called:

Las Vegas, in the Nevada desert; who built up Miami from the Florida marsh; and who carved our heroes into the face of Mount Rushmore.

Americans harnessed electricity, split the atom, and gave the world the telephone and the Internet. We settled the Wild West, won two World Wars, landed American astronauts on the Moon—and one day very soon, we will plant our flag on Mars.

We gave the world the poetry of Walt Whitman, the stories of Mark Twain, the songs of Irving Berlin, the voice of Ella Fitzgerald, the style of Frank Sinatra, the comedy of Bob Hope, the power of the Saturn V rocket, the toughness of the Ford F-150 and the awesome might of the American aircraft carriers.

Americans must never lose sight of this miraculous story. You should never lose sight of it, because nobody has ever done it like we have done it. So today, under the authority vested in me as President of the United States I am announcing the creation of a new monument to the giants of our past. I am signing an executive order to establish the National Garden of American Heroes, a vast outdoor park that will feature the statues of the greatest Americans to ever live.

From this night and from this magnificent place, let us go forward united in our purpose and re-dedicated in our resolve. We will raise the next generation of American patriots. We will write the next thrilling chapter of the American adventure. And we will teach our children to know that they live in a land of legends, that nothing can stop them, and that no one can hold them down. They will know that in America, you can do anything, you can be anything, and together, we can achieve anything.

Uplifted by the titans of Mount Rushmore, we will find unity that no one expected; we will make strides that no one thought possible. This country will be everything that our citizens have hoped for, for so many years, and that our enemies fear—because we will never forget that American freedom exists for American greatness. And that's what we have: American greatness.

Centuries from now, our legacy will be the cities we built, the champions we forged, the good we did, and the monuments we created to inspire us all.

My fellow citizens: America's destiny is in our sights. America's heroes are embedded in our hearts. America's future is in our hands. And ladies and gentlemen: the best is yet to come.

This has been a great honor for the First Lady and myself to be with you. I love your state. I love this country. I'd like to wish everybody a very happy Fourth of July. To all, God bless you, God bless your families, God bless our great military, and God bless America. Thank you very much.

APPENDIX B

COREY LEWANDOWSKI'S TESTIMONY TO HOUSE JUDICIARY COMMITTEE

September 17, 2019

CHAIRMAN NADLER, Ranking Member Collins and members of the committee, good afternoon. I'd like to start off by expressing my hope that today's hearing will be productive in revealing the truth both to the committee and to the American people. For the record and as you likely know, I have already testified before Congress on three separate occasions. I sat at length with the staff of the Special Counsel's office. There too, my time and answers were given freely and without hesitation. I think in one form or another, I've already answered questions for well over 20 hours. So now here I am before the House Judiciary Committee to answer the same questions again.

Just last week this committee, over the objections of the minority, unilaterally changed the rules to make this an impeachment proceeding which is very unfair. However, in the spirit of cooperation, I am prepared to move forward today. I'd like to start by recounting the events that brought us to this point—my story of joining the Trump campaign, working through a historic election and continuing to have the privilege to be part of the greatest political movement in our nation's history.

I present this summary in the interest of truth and transparency to the American people, the very same reason and rationale that this committee offers as the basis of today's hearing. Growing up in a blue-color single-parent family in Lowell, Massachusetts, I learned the value of hard work and that work ethic helped me to put myself through both college and graduate school prior to becoming a Congressional staffer and ultimately a certified peace officer in the state of New Hampshire. However, the world of politics was always a passion and in January of 2015, Donald J. Trump, then a private citizen, hired me to help him explore a possible run for the presidency.

It was an honor and privilege to play a small part of such a historic campaign. The campaign started as a small group of individuals helping Mr. Trump to make the decision in June of 2015 to ride down the golden escalator and seek the Republican nomination for Presidency of the United States.

For more than a year I served as campaign manager to then candidate Trump and his historic campaign where I led a lean and dedicated operation that succeeded in helping him capture the Republican nomination. My job was simple; provide Mr. Trump with my best advice, spend his money like it was my own and give him the support he needed to win. I also set long-term—long-term objectives and managed day to day decisions. I had the privilege and it was a privilege of helping transform the Trump campaign from a dedicated but small make- shift organization to a historical and unprecedented political juggernaut. And I am proud to say Mr. Trump won 38 primaries and caucuses and received more votes than any candidate in the history of the Republican Party all while being outspent most of the way.

The historic campaign helped Mr. Trump secure the republican nomination ultimately the Presidency of the United States. However, since election day, whether there were bad actors at the FBI and the intelligence community or lies coming from members of the current House majority, that there was evidence of collusion, the American people continue to be sold a false narrative with the purpose of undermining the legitimacy of the 2016 election results.

But no matter the size, campaigns are not always the most efficient organizations and while you run in single Congressional districts, just imagine what it's like to lead a national campaign that spans all 50 states of the union. During my time as campaign manager, there were competing interests for the candidate's time and a sea of ideas, some laudable, some sound; a few not so much. Many of which were dismissed out of hand; others were passed on to staffers to be handled.

I also received hundreds of thousands of e-mails, some days with as many as 1,000 e-mails, and unlike Hillary Clinton, I don't think I ever deleted any of those. Many of them were responded to with either one word answers or forwarded to other staffers for additional follow up but throughout it all and to the best of my recollection, I don't ever recall having any conversations with foreign entities, let alone any who were offering to help to manipulate the outcome of an election. As I've said publicly many times, anyone who attempted to illegally impact the outcome of an election should spend the rest of their life in jail. And let me stress this fact, during the 2016 election cycle, Mr. Trump held no elected position; he was not a government official.

Rather the Obama-Biden Administration and the intelligence community overseen by James Clapper, Jim Comey and John Brennan had the responsibility to the American people to ensure the integrity of the 2016 election. I'll leave it to this committee and the American public to decide how successful or not they were in doing their jobs.

Regardless, as a special counsel determined, there was no conspiracy or collusion between the Trump campaign and any foreign governments either on my watch or afterwards. Not surprisingly after the Mueller report was made public, interest in the fake Russia collusion narrative has fallen apart.

In conclusion and it's sad to say, this country has spent over 3 years and $40 million taxpayer dollars on these investigations and it's now clear that the investigation was populated by many Trump haters who had their own agenda—to take down a duly elected president of the United States. As for actual collusion or conspiracy, there was none. What there has been, however, is harassment of this president from the day he won the election. We as a nation would be better served if elected officials like yourself concentrated your efforts to combat the true crises facing our country as opposed to going down rabbit holes like this hearing. Instead of focusing on petty and personal politics, the committee focus on solving the challenges of this generation. Imagine how many people we could help or how many lives we could save.

As I stated earlier, I have voluntarily appeared in front of Congress on three separate occasions and spoken to members of the Special Counsel's office for multiple hours. I will continue to be forth rate—forthright and cooperative and I will be as sincere in my answers as this committee is in its questions.

———————

REP. DOUG COLLINS (R-GA): When you worked on the Trump campaign, and you said this earlier—I just want it to be stated again because we've had these hearings here in the Judiciary Committee didn't seem to take but we'll try again.

Did you engage in collusion, coordination, or conspiracy with the Russians?

COREY LEWANDOWSKI: Never.

COLLINS: Did you observe anyone else doing that?

LEWANDOWSKI: No, Sir.

ACKNOWLEDGMENTS

WE ARE THANKFUL for everyone who helped make this book possible, from our friends in the Trump administration who work every day to support our great president to those who work on the outside of the administration who fight to put America First.

A special thanks goes out to a select few; without their help, this book would not be what it is. Those people include J. T. Mastranadi, August "Augie" Atencio, Michael Boos, Andrew Rittenhouse, and Abigail Lewandowski.

To our editor, Kate Hartson, our publisher, Daisy Blackwell Hutton and the publishing team at Center Street/ Hachette Book Group, and our collaborators, Brian McDonald and Sean McGowan, thank you for bringing this project to life. And to our agent, Tom Winters: we appreciate all you do on our behalf.

INDEX

ABOUT THE AUTHORS

COREY R. LEWANDOWSKI serves as a Senior Advisor to Trump-Pence 2020. He is also president and CEO of Lewandowski Strategic Advisors, LLC. He previously served as campaign manager and chief political strategist to Donald J. Trump for President. Corey serves as a presidential appointee to the Commission on Presidential Scholars. He appears regularly on television and serves as an on-the-record spokesman to major print outlets. He is a contributor to The Hill newspaper and was a visiting fellow at Harvard University. Lewandowski previously served as a certified police officer with the State of New Hampshire, where he lives with his family.

DAVID N. BOSSIE has served as president of Citizens United since 2001. He is currently Senior Advisor to Trump-Pence 2020, and a presidential appointee to the Commission on Presidential Scholars. In 2016, Bossie served as deputy campaign manager for Donald J. Trump for President and then deputy executive director of the Presidential Transition Team. In 2015, Bossie was ranked number two in Politico's top 50 most influential people in American politics. In 2016, he was elected Republican National Committeeman from Maryland. David proudly served as a volunteer firefighter for over 15 years in Maryland where he lives with his wife and their four children.